2004
MASTERS®
ANNUAL

—— III ——

Augusta National Golf Club

WILEY

John Wiley & Sons, Inc.

Augusta National would like to recognize the contributions of writer Dick Mudry and
photographers Sam Greenwood, Rusty Jarrett, and MillerBrown Marketing.

Published by John Wiley & Sons, Inc., Hoboken, New Jersey
Published simultaneously in Canada

Design and production by Navta Associates, Inc.

For general information about our other products and services, please contact our Cus-
tomer Care Department within the United States at (800) 762-2974, outside the United
States at (317) 572-3993 or fax (317) 572-4002.

Wiley also publishes its books in a variety of electronic formats. Some content that
appears in print may not be available in electronic books. For more information about
Wiley products, visit our web site at www.wiley.com.

Library of Congress Cataloging-in-Publication Data:

2004 Masters annual / by Augusta National Golf Club.
    p. cm.
  ISBN 0-471-69009-0 (trade edition) (cloth : alk. paper)
  ISBN 0-471-69010-4 (special edition) (cloth : alk. paper)
 1. Masters Golf Tournament—History.   2. Golf—United States—History.
3. Golfers—Anecdotes.   I. Title: Two thousand four Masters annual.   II. Augusta
National Golf Club.
  GV970.3.M37A16   2004
  796.352'66—dc22

2004011075

Printed in the United States of America

10 9 8 7 6 5 4 3 2 1

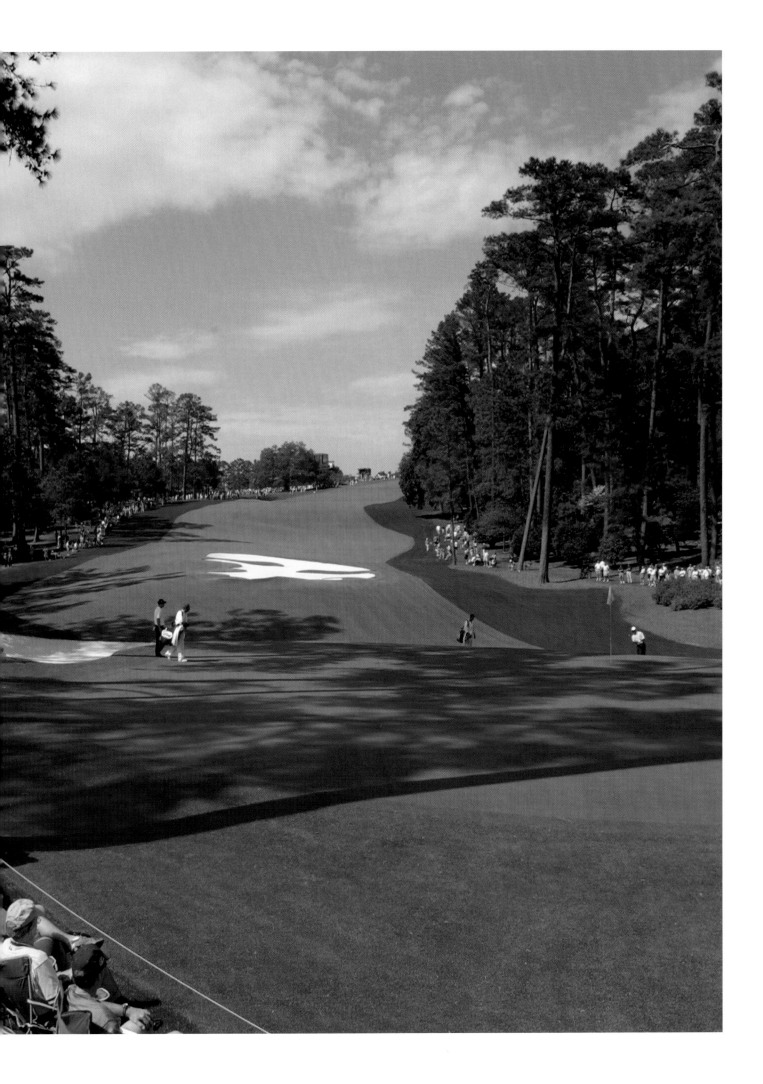

CONTENTS

2004
MASTERS®
ANNUAL

—III—

Framed by a plethora of bunkers, the seventh green presents a difficult target for participants.

Message from the Chairman

—|||—

While the Masters is known for many things—Bobby Jones and Clifford Roberts, the striking beauty of the golf course, and its outstanding players—a display of truly memorable golf on the second nine Sunday may be its trademark.

The likes of Nelson, Hogan, Snead, and later Palmer, Player, Nicklaus battling one another through Amen Corner and beyond holds a special place in Tournament history. A new chapter was added to that book at the 2004 Masters.

Phil Mickelson and Ernie Els traded shot for shot Sunday and neither player blinked. Phil's 18-foot birdie putt at No. 18 proved the difference in one of the most exciting Masters ever. His five birdies over the last seven holes and Ernie's two eagles that final round showed once again that great players can accomplish great things at Augusta National.

The week was also memorable as Arnold Palmer celebrated his 50th consecutive Masters. Many of this Tournament's greatest moments involve Arnold and he will always be linked to Augusta. Someone not present but in our thoughts was caddie Bruce Edwards. We mourn his passing.

I hope you enjoy this year's *Masters Annual,* and on behalf of Augusta National Golf Club I would like to thank everyone for a successful 2004 Masters. I look forward to the 2005 Masters to be held April 4–10.

Hootie Johnson

Palmer Prepares for Masters Finale

—III—

Four-time champion Arnold Palmer prepares to play a record 50th and final Masters Tournament while the rest of the field found a firmer, faster Augusta National than in the past two years.

The drive down Magnolia Lane remains as exciting now as it was the first time, in 1955. It still gives Arnold Palmer, a western Pennsylvania head greenskeeper's son, goose bumps because of the sheer beauty that awaits him at the end of the road.

It is a place of wonderful, lasting memories, four Masters wins, and many more near misses at victory.

Can it really be 50 years since Arnold Daniel Palmer first played in the Masters Tournament?

Can it really be 40 years since Palmer won the last of his four Masters?

Can it really be the end of golf's most charismatic player at a place he so cherishes?

Those questions rattled through the minds of players and patrons all over the world when the 68th Masters Tournament began.

The 2004 Masters was to be Palmer's adieu, at least in the competitive vein.

Of course, Palmer will enjoy the nuances of the rolling hills and tree-lined fairways as an Augusta National Golf Club member in the future.

But Arnie without the Masters on his schedule seems incomprehensible.

"I guess Arnold has meant more to the Masters Tournament than anyone," said Chairman Hootie Johnson before the Tournament began. "He's meant more to golf. He's an exciting player. He's even exciting at [age] 74 whether he's going off the first tee or playing the 10th hole."

Palmer's patron-friendly demeanor has enamored generations of golfers and non-golfers alike.

Even today's players revere the people's player.

"Just a legend, a living legend," said three-time Masters champion Tiger Woods of Palmer's legacy in the game. "If it wasn't for Arnold, golf wouldn't be as popular as it is now. You know he's the one who basically brought it to the forefront on TV. If it wasn't for him and his excitement, his flare, the way he played, golf probably would not have had that type of excitement."

Palmer's dashing good looks and go-for-broke play on the golf course brought the game to a variety of cultures and countries.

Arnold Palmer strides down the
fairway in his final Masters.

That began in 1958, three years after his first Masters Tournament.

It was in 1958 that Palmer, aided by an eagle at the par-5 13th hole, catapulted himself to his first major title and super-stardom all in the same four days.

Golf would never be the same, and Augusta National Golf Club would be Palmer's soul mate, a place where he felt most at home.

Palmer may have won 92 times around the world, but none were more cherished than his four Masters wins. He also won in 1960, 1962, and 1964.

"I'm going to miss coming and playing in the Masters as I have for 50 years," said Palmer before his farewell began.

"You do anything that long, it's like get-ting married. It's been great. It's been 50 great years."

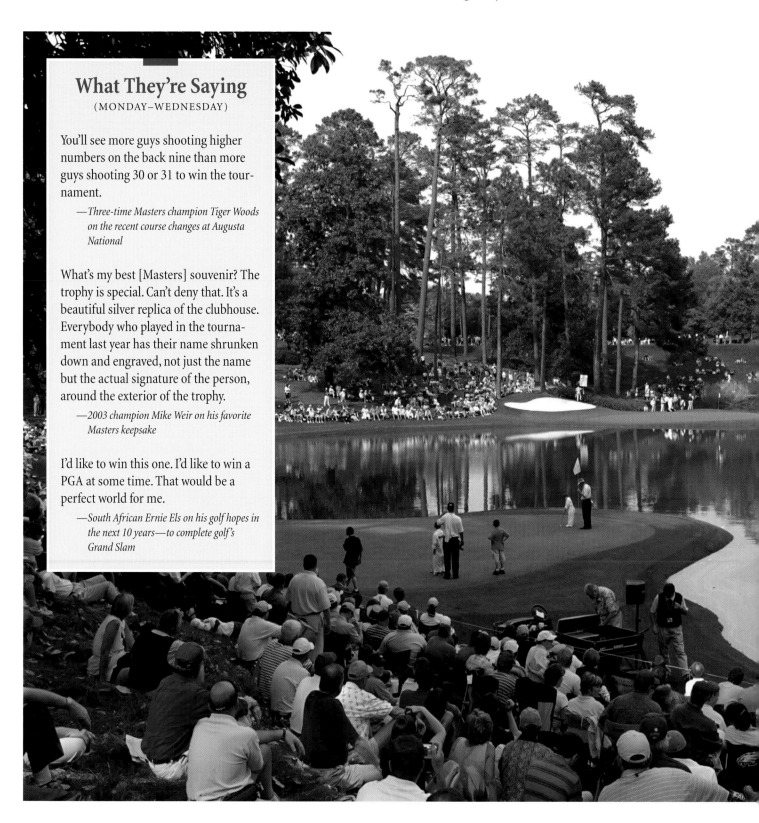

What They're Saying
(MONDAY–WEDNESDAY)

You'll see more guys shooting higher numbers on the back nine than more guys shooting 30 or 31 to win the tour-nament.

> —*Three-time Masters champion Tiger Woods on the recent course changes at Augusta National*

What's my best [Masters] souvenir? The trophy is special. Can't deny that. It's a beautiful silver replica of the clubhouse. Everybody who played in the tourna-ment last year has their name shrunken down and engraved, not just the name but the actual signature of the person, around the exterior of the trophy.

> —*2003 champion Mike Weir on his favorite Masters keepsake*

I'd like to win this one. I'd like to win a PGA at some time. That would be a perfect world for me.

> —*South African Ernie Els on his golf hopes in the next 10 years—to complete golf's Grand Slam*

Age has been the only foe that Palmer cannot defeat. But, said Palmer, that doesn't diminish his enjoyment of the Masters.

"Thursday and Friday will be fun for me," he said, relishing the prospect of having his family and many friends—in addition to his grandson Sam Saunders as his caddie—at a record 50th Masters.

"I suppose it's a bittersweet-type situation."

Patrons enjoy the golf and the serene surroundings of the Par 3 Contest.

Phil Mickelson
(MONDAY–WEDNESDAY)

As the Masters Tournament began its run-up to the first round, no one was more anxious for play to begin than Phil Mickelson.

Mickelson hoped to become the second left-handed player in as many years to don a prestigious Green Jacket when the week is over, joining Mike Weir.

And who's to argue with the 33-year-old Rancho Santa Fe, California, resident?

His record—particularly in the past five Masters—has been stellar.

Mickelson has finished no worse than tied for seventh over the Augusta National Golf Club since 1999. Moreover, the 12-year professional has finished third each of the past three years, narrowly missing his first major title.

So when Mickelson came to the former Fruitland Nurseries this April, he did so with great optimism.

"I have entered this Tournament the last few years believing that I had very good chances," said Mickelson in the days before the start of play. "This year I certainly feel like I have a very good chance. I think what's been nice is that I've played well week in and week out. I've played very consistently, which is something I certainly didn't do last year, but I was striving to do that this year."

In eight events leading up to the Masters, Mickelson had won the 2004 Bob Hope Chrysler Classic, and finished in the top 10 seven times.

He would like nothing better than to make the 2004 Masters his first major championship after a series of near misses.

"I've really enjoyed the challenge of trying to win a major," said Mickelson. "Although I haven't broken through and won, I enjoy all the challenges in my life. It is a fun challenge to play a course that is so penalizing under such tough conditions, to try to shoot the lowest score, manage your game the best, be patient, all those things that are necessary to win. I know I haven't done it yet, but I've been close a number of times, and I think that when I finally do break through, it will be that much more rewarding for going through the difficulties of the last 10 years of trying it and not doing it."

The 2004 Tournament may be Mickelson's best chance for victory.

He comes to Augusta National Golf Club in, perhaps, his best playing form ever.

And Augusta National has been kind to him in the past.

His record only reinforces his position as a Masters favorite.

His scoring average is 71.14 in 11 previous outings. He's a cumulative 36 under par and has 13 rounds in the 60s.

In each of the past three years, the 12-year professional has been within a whisper of victory.

A break here or there and Mickelson might already have been a Masters champion.

"I have a lot more confidence that I'll be there come the weekend or that I'll have an opportunity," said Mickelson of the 72 holes of golf ahead.

"I'm playing well enough to get into contention without having to do anything extraordinary."

First time Masters invitee Stephen Leaney of Australia blasts from a bunker during a practice round.

Numbers tell only a part of Palmer's Masters success. But after 49 appearances, they must be noted.

He's played 148 competitive rounds, finishing 72 holes 25 times.

There are nine top-five finishes on his resume, totaling 11,012 strokes over 2,664 holes played. Total up the distance Palmer has walked at the Masters, and it's nearly 600 eye-popping miles coming into 2004.

Yet his legacy will be measured in more than simple numbers. Palmer's legacy is what he leaves behind for the game.

His peers know it only too well.

"There's many, many great players before Arnie," said Northern Ireland's Darren Clarke, "but the following he had and the support he had brought a lot of people into the game of golf. It certainly helped make the game grow bigger and bigger. You know, [it's] sad to see him playing his last one, but he's been an amazing man for a long, long time."

"Great champion that he is, he's kept coming back," said South African Ernie Els of Palmer's impact not only at the Masters but also in the game of golf. "You know he's put a lot of majors and a lot of golf tournaments right on the map in the world. He's been a great ambassador for the game."

That attitude, said Palmer, has served him well and came from his father, Deke.

"What he taught me was manners, to be polite and to treat other people like I would like to be treated," Palmer said.

Be a gentleman, Deke Palmer told his son, in a gentleman's game.

Ask any amateur player, past or present, who they most enjoy playing with at the Masters Tournament and a likely answer is "Arnold Palmer."

"Every amateur . . . when they get in the field, the first call they make is to his representatives trying to get a practice round with him," said Phil Mickelson of his 1991 Masters practice round with Palmer.

"What I remember about that was we had a little competition with our two playing partners. One of them was against Lanny [Wadkins] and Tom Watson. And boy, on 8 and 9 Arnie made birdies. He gave it the Arnie fist pump, gave that grin to the crowd, and people loved it. I think that was a glimpse in his eye of the competitive Arnold Palmer when he used to make the charge and win. It was an awesome sight to behold."

Palmer still has the twinkle in his eye on the golf course, and Augusta National is no different. He is still a dreamer, someone who believes he can catch lightning in a bottle someday, and today may just be that day. Call him an eternal optimist.

He was asked how he expected Friday to unfold, given the state of his game and the emotional day it will surely be for him in his final walk up to the 18th hole.

"I know exactly how I want Friday to unfold, no question," said the golf icon. "I want to see what my starting time is on Saturday."

The rest of the 93-player field would love to see the four-time champion around for the weekend, too, just as they loved seeing

Keeping notes on the course is all part of being a caddie at the Masters.

What They're Writing
(MONDAY–WEDNESDAY)

Arnold Palmer Day began with the 74-year-old, 50-year Masters veteran slowly driving up Magnolia Lane in his white Cadillac.

Hey, when you're The King, you arrive at work in style.

As he emerged from the driver's seat, flashbulbs popped, video cameras whirred, and fans got markers ready for autographs.

Hey, when you're the leader of Arnie's Army, your arrival sets off waves of commotion.

And when it's the last week of your Masters Tournament career, you savor every step along the way.

—*Josh Katzowitz,* Augusta Chronicle

While the other top dogs in Georgia head into the week playing less than their best, Phil Mickelson is the steadiest player in golf, words that have rarely been spoken. After enduring a dismal 2003 that was filled with zero triumphs and one near-tragedy, Mickelson has emerged as the pick of the populace to win his first major at Augusta National.

Mickelson, who has finished third three years in a row at Augusta, has throttled down his attack, is generally keeping the ball out of the magnolias and azaleas and could finally snap his 0-for-45 famine in the major championships.

—*Steve Elling,* Orlando Sentinel

Ten years ago, Mike Weir wasn't thinking of winning green jackets and planning the Champions Dinner menu at Augusta National. Ten years ago, the Canadian simply was trying to make a decent living playing golf, unsure if that ever was going to happen.

There was the time he was playing in a lower-rung event in Indonesia in the mid-1990s. He was taking a cab to the course when the car broke down and there was no caddy to turn to for help.

"I carried my bag through all this muddy water, hitchhiking back to the golf course and made a 9 on a par-3 to shoot 80," Weir said. "I think probably then I had a tough time thinking I would win the Masters."

—*Craig Dolch,* Palm Beach Post

If you're a golf fan, I have one piece of advice for you: Before you die, visit Augusta National Golf Club during the Masters. Trust me. The golf course in heaven won't be this nice.

I don't care how hard it is to get tickets. . . . Do whatever it takes to get on a plane. Tell your spouse you're just running out to get some bread. But get yourself down here.

Now, I've been to some impressive tracks. I've visited the Pebble Beach courses, and I've played Oakland Hills and the Plantation Course at Kapalua. But after walking among Augusta's towering pines and blushing azaleas on a sun-kissed day, those other courses just sort of blend in.

—*Carlos Monarrez,* Detroit Free Press

Three-time champion Gary Player and his grandson enjoyed a lighter moment during the Par 3 Contest.

him play in the Par 3 Contest Wednesday, with Woods and former Masters champion Mark O'Meara.

Ireland's Padraig Harrington won the Par 3 Contest, defeating Eduardo Romero. Harrington birdied the third playoff hole with a 2½-foot putt to claim the title.

Tiger Woods also tied Harrington and Romero with scores of 23, but a previous commitment prevented Woods from competing in the playoff.

Harrington shared the 2003 rain-interrupted Par 3 Contest title with David Toms.

A total of four holes-in-one were made, bringing the total made in the event to 55.

Defending champion Mike Weir, Phillip Price, Woods, and Jay Haas made aces in the Par 3 Contest, which began in 1960.

But the players have to worry that their own games are ready for a course that probably will play the most difficult in several years.

The field faces only two changes to the layout that redesigned and lengthened tees on nine holes in 2002 and made several other fairway and bunker changes to stretch the course to 7,290 yards.

A total of 36 pine trees were added to the right side of the 11th fairway to require more precise tee shots at the 490-yard, par-4 hole. The green at the 510-yard, par-5 13th was rebuilt, and a heating and cooling system was installed under the putting surface.

With cool mornings yielding to warm, sunny days, the Masters Tournament will show a different face for the first time in at least two years, perhaps longer.

Without rain leading up to the opening round, the par-72 layout will play firm and fast.

That will require more accurate drives in the fairway to set up more precise irons into the greens. Dry conditions will make the undulating greens more lethal, too.

"We're big-time excited and the players I've talked to are excited about the course conditions," said Will F. Nicholson Jr., Chairman of the Competition Committees.

It will require players to control their shots more precisely.

Invitees Kirk Triplett, left, and Tim Herron, center, were helped by three young caddies and a veteran at the Par 3 Contest.

MASTERS HISTORY

15 Years Ago: Nick Faldo defeated Scott Hoch in a playoff. Hoch missed a two-foot par putt at the first extra hole, while Faldo made a 25-foot birdie putt at No. 11 to win the Masters.

20 Years Ago: Texan Ben Crenshaw won the first of two Masters with a final round of 4-under-par 68 and 72-hole total of 277, two strokes better than Tom Watson. Crenshaw, who won his second Masters in 1995, started the final round two strokes behind leader Tom Kite.

25 Years Ago: The Masters first sudden-death playoff. Since then there have been five playoffs, and Nick Faldo is the only player to have won more than once. Faldo won playoffs in 1989 and 1990.

50 Years Ago: In one of the most famous playoffs in Masters history, Sam Snead defeated Ben Hogan 70 to 71 to win the last of his three Green Jackets. Snead's score of one-over-par 289 remains tied for the highest winning score in Masters history.

60 Years Ago: Augusta National Golf Club was closed and the Masters was cancelled due to World War II. The Tournament was suspended from 1943 to 1945.

70 Years Ago: The Masters begins what would become a series of innovative firsts. Spectator mounds, gallery roping, the over-under scoring system, scoreboards throughout the course, and the first overseas golf broadcast were introduced to professional golf at Augusta National Golf Club.

"Last year, if you short-sided yourself with as much rain as we had, the greens were soft enough that you could maybe get the ball up and down from the wrong side of the hole," said 2003 champion Mike Weir. "This year you're not going to really have that option. You're going to have to be on the correct side of the hole."

"I also like it playing hard and fast because I've played this event when it's been hard and fast in the past," said Mickelson, a third-place finisher each of the past three years. "I have a pretty good idea of where I can hit shots to certain pins and where I can't save shots."

Knowing that and doing that, as Mickelson knows, are two different things.

So does 2000 Masters champion Vijay Singh.

"This is, to me, the hardest test of golf we play," said Singh of the examination the Masters puts players through. "It requires the whole package. You can't come here with one part of the game missing. You're just not going to function."

With all those variables staring the best players in the world in the face and the drama of Arnold Palmer's good-bye sure to add additional poignancy to the proceedings, the Tournament was sure to be another one for the record books. ∎

Augusta native Charles Howell III, left, and three-time champion Tiger Woods shared a conversation during a practice round.

Masters veteran Jay Haas sharpened his putting stroke leading up to the first round.

China's Lian-Wei Zhang

(MONDAY–WEDNESDAY)

The first time the international golf world saw him was eight years ago, in his hometown of Shenzhen, China.

That's when the 1995 World Cup of Golf traveled to China, just a stone's throw from vibrant and hectic Hong Kong.

Well, Lian-Wei Zhang was a rookie pro in those days, a player in a country where golf was in its infancy. He and the Chinese team finished near the bottom of the international field, but the experience gave golf in China a major shot in the arm.

So when the 68th Masters began, Lian-Wei Zhang had come a long, long way.

Zhang, via a special invitation from the Masters Committee, joined the elite field at Augusta National Golf Club.

At 38 and from a country with well over 1 billion people, Zhang was the first Chinese golfer to play in the Masters.

He received the invitation because of "his proven ability on the European Tour and in Asia," Chairman Hootie Johnson said. "We felt it good for the game of golf to extend a hand to the most populous nation in the world. He is a good golfer and we thought it was entirely appropriate."

Zhang earned his invitation by becoming the first Chinese golfer to win on the European Tour. He birdied the final hole of the 2003 Caltex Masters to defeat South African Ernie Els by one stroke.

Zhang also won the 2003 China Open and in 2002 successfully defended his Macau Open title. He was second in 2003 on the Asian Tour's Order of Merit.

Past Par 3 Contest CHAMPS

Year	Player	Score
1960	Sam Snead	23
1961	Deane Beman	22
1962	Bruce Crampton	22
1963*	George Bayer	23
1964	Labron Harris Jr.	23
1965	Art Wall Jr.	20
1966	Terry Dill	22
1967*	Arnold Palmer	23
1968	Bob Rosburg	22
1969*	Bob Lunn	23
1970	Harold Henning	21
1971*	Dave Stockton	23
1972	Steve Melnyk	23
1973	Gay Brewer	20
1974*	Sam Snead	23
1975*	Isao Aoki	23
1976	Jay Haas	21
1977*	Tom Weiskopf	23
1978*	Lou Graham	22
1979	Joe Inman Jr.	23
1980	Johnny Miller	23
1981	Isao Aoki	22
1982*	Tom Watson	23
1983	Hale Irwin	22
1984	Tommy Aaron	22
1985	Hubert Green	22
1986*	Gary Koch	23
1987	Ben Crenshaw	22
1988	Tsuneyuki Nakajima	24
1989*	Bob Gilder	22
1990	Raymond Floyd	23
1991*	Rocco Mediate	24
1992	Davis Love III	22
1993	Chip Beck	21
1994	Vijay Singh	22
1995*	Hal Sutton	23
1996*	Jay Haas	22
1997*	Sandy Lyle	22
1998	Sandy Lyle	24
1999	Joe Durant	22
2000*	Chris Perry	23
2001	David Toms	22
2002*	Nick Price	22
2003+	Padraig Harrington	
	David Toms	21
2004*	Padraig Harrington	23

*Won in playoff +Tied

2004 Masters Tournament Invitees

Number after each name indicates the basis of qualification. See qualifications on next page.
#Denotes first Masters. *Denotes amateur.

Tommy Aaron (1)
Robert Allenby (Australia) (14,16, 17)
Stuart Appleby (Australia) (14, 15, 16, 17)
George Archer (1)
#Briny Baird (14)
Seve Ballesteros (Spain) (1)
Rich Beem (4, 10, 16)
Thomas Bjorn (Denmark) (12, 16, 17)
Gay Brewer (1)
Jack Burke (1)
Jonathan Byrd (10)
Angel Cabrera (Argentina) (10)
Chad Campbell (13, 14, 15, 16, 17)
Michael Campbell (New Zealand) (16)
#Paul Casey (England) (16, 17)
Billy Casper (1)
Alex Cejka (Germany) (13, 16, 17)
K. J. Choi (Korea) (10, 14, 16, 17)
Stewart Cink (14, 17)
Tim Clark (South Africa) (10, 13)
Darren Clarke (N. Ireland) (16, 17)
Charles Coody (1)
Fred Couples (1, 14, 16, 17)
Ben Crenshaw (1)
#Ben Curtis (3, 16, 17)
John Daly (15)
#Brian Davis (England) (17)
Chris DiMarco (14, 16, 17)
David Duval (3)
Ernie Els (South Africa) (3, 10, 11, 14, 16, 17)
Bob Estes (14, 16)
Nick Faldo (England) (1)
Brad Faxon (14, 16, 17)
#*Nick Flanagan (Australia) (6-A)
Steve Flesch (14, 17)

Raymond Floyd (1)
Doug Ford (1)
Fred Funk (14, 16, 17)
Jim Furyk (2, 10, 14, 16, 17)
Sergio Garcia (Spain) (16, 17)
Bob Goalby (1)
Retief Goosen (South Africa) (2, 10, 14, 16, 17)
Jay Haas (14, 16, 17)
#Todd Hamilton (17)
Padraig Harrington (Ireland) (16, 17)
Tim Herron (14, 16)
Charles Howell III (14, 16, 17)
Trevor Immelman (South Africa) (17)
Toshi Izawa (Japan) (16)
#Fredrik Jacobson (Sweden) (11, 16, 17)
Jonathan Kaye (14, 15, 16, 17)
Jerry Kelly (14, 16, 17)
Bernhard Langer (Germany) (1)
Paul Lawrie (Scotland) (3, 10)
#Stephen Leaney (Australia) (11, 16, 17)
Justin Leonard (14, 16, 17)
#J. L. Lewis (14)
Peter Lonard (Australia) (16, 17)
Davis Love III (5, 10, 12, 14, 15, 16, 17)
Sandy Lyle (Scotland) (1)
Jeff Maggert (10)
Shigeki Maruyama (Japan) (14, 16, 17)
Len Mattiace (10)
Rocco Mediate (14, 16, 17)
#Shaun Micheel (4, 14, 16, 17)
Phil Mickelson (10, 14, 15, 16, 17)
Larry Mize (1)
Colin Montgomerie (Scotland) (16, 17)
Byron Nelson (1)

Jack Nicklaus (1)
José Maria Olazabal (Spain) (1, 10)
Mark O'Meara (1, 10)
Arnold Palmer (1)
Craig Parry (Australia) (17)
Craig Perks (New Zealand) (5)
Kenny Perry (11, 14, 16, 17)
#Tim Petrovic (14)
Gary Player (South Africa) (1)
#Ian Poulter (England) (16, 17)
Nick Price (Zimbabwe) (11, 14, 16, 17)
#Phillip Price (Wales) (16)
Chris Riley (14, 16, 17)
John Rollins (14)
Eduardo Romero (Argentina) (16)
Justin Rose (England) (11)
Adam Scott (Australia) (5, 15, 16, 17)
Vijay Singh (Fiji) (1, 10, 12, 14, 15, 16, 17)
Jeff Sluman (14)
#*Nathan Smith (9)
#*Brandt Snedeker (8)
Craig Stadler (1)
David Toms (4, 10, 11, 14, 16, 17)
Kirk Triplett (14, 17)
Bob Tway (14, 16, 17)
Scott Verplank (10, 14, 16, 17)
Tom Watson (1)
Mike Weir (Canada) (1, 11, 14, 15, 16, 17)
#*Casey Wittenberg (6-B)
*Gary Wolstenholme (England) (7)
Tiger Woods (1, 2, 3, 4, 10, 12, 14, 15, 16, 17)
Ian Woosnam (Wales) (1)
Lian-Wei Zhang (China)
Fuzzy Zoeller(1)

Darren Clarke of Northern Ireland takes in the splendor of the 10th hole during a practice round.

For the second year in a row Ireland's Padraig Harrington was the winner in the Par 3 Contest. Harrington won a three-hole playoff with Eduardo Romero. In 2003 Harrington and David Toms shared the title.

How They Qualified

1 Masters Tournament champions (lifetime)

2 U.S. Open champions (honorary, noncompeting after five years)

3 British Open champions (honorary, noncompeting after five years)

4 PGA champions (honorary, noncompeting after five years)

5 Winners of The Players Championship (three years)

6 Current US Amateur champion (6-A) (honorary, non-competing after one year) and the runner-up (6-B) to the current U.S. Amateur champion

7 Current British Amateur champion (honorary, noncom-peting after one year)

8 Current U.S. Amateur Public Links champion

9 Current U.S. Mid-Amateur champion

10 The first 16 players, including ties, in the 2003 Masters Tournament

11 The first eight players, including ties, in the 2003 U.S. Open Championship

12 The first four players, including ties, in the 2003 British Open Championship

13 The first four players, including ties, in the 2003 PGA Championship

14 The 40 leaders on the Final Official PGA Tour Money List for 2003

15 The 10 leaders on the Official PGA Tour Money List published during the week prior to the 2004 Masters Tournament

16 The 50 leaders on the Final Official World Golf Ranking for 2003

17 The 50 leaders on the Official World Golf Ranking published during the week prior to the 2004 Masters Tournament.

The Masters Committee, at its discretion, also invites International players not otherwise qualified.

Rose Makes Most of Birdie Chances

———|||———

England's 23-year-old Justin Rose, the youngest professional in the field, took advantage of opening and closing birdies for a 67 to take the first-round lead while Chris DiMarco and veteran Jay Haas trailed by two strokes.

After three days of sunny skies and warm temperatures, the weather changed on the opening round of the Masters.

Less than an hour after first-round play began, rain showers sent players and patrons alike reaching for rainwear and umbrellas.

The showers, intermittent throughout the day, finally suspended play at 4:09 P.M., when heavy rain and lightning were detected in the Augusta area. Play was resumed more than two hours later.

And when Chairman of the Competition Committees, Will F. Nicholson Jr., finally suspended play for the day at 7:45 P.M., a total of 18 players, including former champions Jack Nicklaus, Tiger Woods, Mike Weir, Mark O'Meara, and José Maria Olazabal, were to finish their rounds the following morning.

So what was the end result of the first round?

A 23-year-old Englishman playing in only his second Masters, and someone familiar with the wet, damp conditions of the PGA European Tour, was atop the leader board.

Justin Rose, who finished fourth as an amateur in the 1998 British Open, claimed the lead with a five-under-par 67. Rose's six-birdie, one-bogey round left him two shots ahead of 35-year-old Chris DiMarco, who recorded a hole-in-one on the par-3 sixth hole, and 50-year-old Jay Haas, who is playing in his 21st Masters. Rose and DiMarco played in the same grouping. They were the third starting time of the day.

Four players stood at two-under-par 70 once play was completed, including Northern Ireland's Darren Clark, a first-round leader in 2003 who eventually tied for 28th place; three-time major championship winner Ernie Els of South Africa, Czechoslovakian-born Alex Cejka, and 30-year-old Chris Riley of Las Vegas.

Seven more broke par with rounds of 71 on a day when patience with the weather conditions and the difficulty of the golf course was a key element of success.

There were only 14 subpar rounds, but plenty of wide scoring swings as well.

Justin Rose of England was spot-on with his irons, shooting a five-under-par 67 for a two-stroke lead.

HOLE OF THE DAY

(ROUND ONE)

HOLE NO. 5

Name: Magnolia

Par 4; 455 yards

This uphill dogleg left hole had fangs put back in it following the 2002 Masters. The hole was lengthened, and two bunkers at the dogleg now forced a 315-yard carry. When the first round was played, it was a ferocious foe. Among 93 players, there were 53 pars, 34 bogeys, and four double bogeys for a hole that played a cumulative 40 over par and averaged 4.43 strokes. Defending Masters champion Mike Weir and three-time Masters champion Tiger Woods each made double-bogey sixes. Only two-time Masters champion Ben Crenshaw and Masters rookie Ben Curtis birdied the hole, where the green slopes down to the front and a back bunker catches shots hit too long.

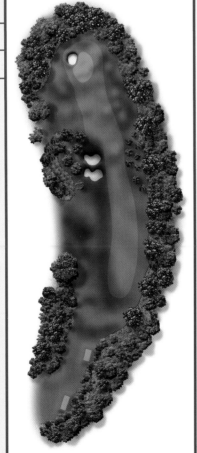

When his approach shot flew long at the 455-yard, par-4 fifth hole, Tiger Woods finished in the magnolias and made a double bogey.

PGA Tour veteran Kirk Triplett, for example, shot 71, including a second nine of 32 with four birdies. He also made a triple-bogey eight at the par-5 second hole for nines of 39–32.

Weir, the defending champion, struggled mightily, too. Standing one-over-par after 12 holes, the Canadian finished bogey, par, double bogey, bogey, bogey, bogey for 79 and stood in danger of missing the 36-hole cut.

Japan's Shigeki Maruyama struggled as well, carding nines of 36–46. He made a quintuple-bogey eight at the par-3 12th hole, hitting one tee shot in the water, and needed three shots to extricate himself from a green-side bunker; he also had a triple-bogey seven at the par-4 17th hole. Maruyama's second nine included two birdies, one par, four bogeys, and two "others".

The subplots of the opening round also included two poignant moments, each dia-metrically opposed from the other.

Along every fairway and beside every green, Masters patrons stood and applauded loudly every time Arnold Palmer came their way.

Despite a less than pleasing score, Palmer was appreciative of the reception. "It's been wonderful," he said. "If I can get through tomorrow I'll be complete."

Former champion Tom Watson's day, however, was not as happy as Palmer's.

Before teeing off, Watson was informed that his longtime caddie Bruce Edwards had died that morning of Lou Gehrig's disease

South African Tim Clark took a mighty swing in the water hazard fronting the par-5 13th green and then watched his shot fly onto the putting surface.

What They're Writing

(ROUND ONE)

Justin Rose, at 23, has known more golfing highs and lows than most experience in a career.

As a 17-year-old amateur, he finished fourth in the 1998 Open while, a week later, he embarked on a run of 21 missed cuts. Yesterday, after a 2003 season in which he failed to follow up on his four wins of the previous year, the gifted Englishman was at the top of the Masters leader board with a five-under-par 67.

—*Lewine Mair,* London Telegraph

The first time Justin Rose dared to look at the leader board, he was walking off the 18th green with applause in his ears. What the big red numbers told him was that he had completed his round in five strokes under par, and was leading the Masters. It was still early in the day, of course.

Rose had gone off in the third group, while most of the big guns were still thinking about breakfast. By the time he finished his round, Ernie Els and Tiger Woods had yet to begin their day's work.

—*Richard Williams,* London Guardian

On a gloomy, rainy day made bleaker by the death of Bruce Edwards, longtime caddie for former Masters champion Tom Watson, Justin Rose emerged as a surprise contender for a Green Jacket.

But Rose, who highlighted a strong foreign contingent Thursday with a five-under-par 67 on a day when just three players broke 70, will have to defy odds to win this major championship Sunday.

—*Jerry Potter,* USA TODAY

They didn't stop play for afternoon tea—it was a thunderstorm that suspended tee time at 4:09 P.M. local time—yet Thursday's first round of the 2004 Masters was *so* English.

The sun peeped in and out all day, the rain was off and on, and 23-year-old Justin Rose, by way of Fleet, Hampshire, shot a five-under-par 67 to take a two-shot lead into a somewhat soggy clubhouse.

Jolly good.

—*Chris Dufresne,* Los Angeles Times

in Ponte Vedra Beach, Florida. Edwards was diagnosed with the crippling disease 15 months earlier.

Watson's 4-over-par 76 was tinged with deep grief, but he believed that Edwards' bubbly spirit was with him during his 31st Masters.

"I think he's not with us in body anymore," Watson said of his friend/caddie, "but I can tell you he's with us in spirit. If you ever ran across him, you knew what a genuine person he was and what a wonderful way he had with his words."

Edwards caddied for Watson in the 2003 Masters.

Lit by the glow of the sunset, Ernie Els drives at the 15th hole.

2000 champion Vijay Singh was keenly focused on his shot to the par-3 12th hole.

The day, however, was a Rose(y) one for England's next potential great player.

Rose, who turned pro after that 1998 British Open showing, has known many highs and lows in his career.

He missed 21 cuts in his first professional year and failed to qualify for the PGA European Tour in 1998. Rose had been one of England's most promising amateurs, a winner of the English Boys Stroke Play Championship and the St. Andrews Links Trophy, and he was a member of the Walker Cup team in 1997.

The 6-foot, 2½-inch Rose finally fulfilled his potential in 2002, when he won twice in Europe. In nine starts worldwide in 2004,

Jay Haas took dead aim at the flag on the ninth green during his round of three-under-par 69.

Jay Haas
(ROUND ONE)

At age 50, Jay Haas remains an inveterate dreamer.

His dream is to follow in the footsteps of his uncle, Bob Goalby, the 1968 Masters champion.

"My dream is to have a locker with him in the Champions Locker Room," said Haas after a first-round three-under-par 69. "That's something that I've thought a lot about over the years." Goalby, now 75 and coming off knee surgery, has been Haas' mentor. He's been his nephew's swing coach and his eyes and ears. And one of these days Haas would like to earn a Green Jacket, too.

That would be still another first. No two winners have ever been related.

"When he won in 1968, I was 14," said Haas after a four-birdie, one-bogey round.

"I did not pay a lot of attention. There wasn't a lot of golf on TV. It wasn't mainstream, like it is now. I did not realize at all what it meant to him to win this tournament. But I knew that everyone talked about it after the fact that next year."

Only after he turned professional in 1976 did Haas realize the full extent of what winning the Masters means.

Yes, there have been nine PGA Tour victories for the South Carolinian.

Yes, there have been wonderful personal moments.

Yes, there have been near misses at Augusta National Golf Club, including top-five finishes in 1985, 1994, and 1995.

But a Masters victory would be sweet, especially at age 50, said Haas. If it becomes so, he would be the oldest ever to win the Grand Slam event.

It would mean more, Haas said, after missing the cut in 2003.

"I guess at this point last year, I was in the top 10 of the money list and felt like I was going to continue and probably be able to finish in the top 40 to get back in here, and I was certainly glad about that," he said.

Haas was relieved to be back in 2004 because his performance last year left him wanting another chance.

Haas shot 79–76 and missed the 36-hole cut for only the third time in 20 starts.

"I played horribly last year and kind of matched the weather, I suppose. I was disappointed in that," he said.

Given his reprieve, Haas wants to make the most of his 21st Masters.

With one caveat, Haas thinks his experience will help.

Can a guy with the experience a 50-year-old holds win?

"I've made all of the mistakes there are to make here, hit it in all the wrong places, and so I know where not to go. But even knowing where to go, I don't always hit it where I'm looking," he said.

Haas has, however, been looking for that coveted Green Jacket for his résumé.

And his uncle hasn't let him try on the Masters Green Jacket.

"No, it doesn't fit me," he said, smiling. "I need my own, I think."

Rose's best finishes are a T23 at the South African Airways Open and a T24 at the Bay Hill Invitational.

The youngster was ecstatic about his beginning.

"It's a dream start," he said of a round that began with two birdies and included others at Nos. 9, 13, 17, and 18, along with a lone bogey at the downhill and difficult par-4 11th.

"Just to get off to a birdie, birdie start was—you know—it gets you into the tournament from the word go. It makes your day much, much easier."

Rose would go on to play nearly flawless golf save for two three-putt greens among his 32 putts.

He hit 17 of 18 greens in regulation and 10 of 14 fairways despite the uneven weather conditions.

"You can always say it could have been better," he said, uttering a golfer's common lament.

"The only one I could really sort of complain about was the fact that I three-putted from a pretty good birdie chance at 11."

DiMarco, a 10-year veteran of the PGA Tour and a three-time winner, had his own moments during the day.

Spain's Sergio Garcia, left, and two-time champion Bernhard Langer, like many in the field, dodged raindrops during first round play.

Lian-Wei Zhang of China was pointing at his target at the par-5 eighth hole.

Tiger Woods was disappointed after nearly holing out at the 17th hole.

Shot of the Day
(ROUND ONE)

Nothing tickled Chris DiMarco more than winning an engraved large crystal bowl in the first round of the Masters.

The bowl is awarded to the player making a hole-in-one, and DiMarco did that at the 198-yard, par-3 sixth hole with a 5-iron.

"I finally got some crystal," said DiMarco of a shot that landed a couple of feet short of the hole and barely trickled in. DiMarco shot a three-under-par 69, a score that left him tied for second.

It was his fourth competitive career hole-in-one and the 15th in Masters history. DiMarco's hole-in-one was the fourth on the downhill, amphitheater hole, the first since Charles Coody in 1972.

What's the most aced hole at Augusta National Golf Club? Including 2004, it's the 170-yard 16th, where nine holes-in-one have been made, two in consecutive groups this year.

He jump-started things with the hole-in-one at No. 6 and made a birdie at the par-5 15th hole. Other than that, pars dotted the rest of his card.

DiMarco's fourth competitive hole-in-one was energizing, he said.

"Every one of us knows when we play that hole, it is probably the hardest hole position on that hole [to get a shot] up top," he said of the pin location, 15 paces on from the front of the narrow green and near the right edge.

"I hit one of those shots that was just perfect. You could see in the air it was the right distance."

The 5-iron from 198 yards, played in heavy rain, bounced twice and trickled into the cup. DiMarco hit 13 of 18 greens in regulation but only eight of 14 fairways. A mere 29 putts made up for his sometimes loose driving.

In his fourth Masters, DiMarco has past experience to draw on. He was

Northern Ireland's Darren Clarke surveys his putt on the eighth hole.

the first- and second-round leader in 2001 but eventually finished tied for 10th with a final round of 74. He tied for 12th in 2002 and played only one round last year.

DiMarco believes his modest success at the Masters is because of his respect for and love of the event.

"You know, there's something special about it," he said. "Every green you go out there, you feel something. The aura of the place is magnificent."

Haas feels the same way. His uncle, Bob Goalby, was the 1968 Masters champion, so he knows the special feeling a champion lives with daily. And at 50, Haas is playing some of the best golf of his life, part of it because of improved equipment and part of it due to being in better physical shape.

"I'm better now than I've been at certain times of my career, certainly. I'm playing very consistently. I'm doing a lot of good things, but I think I'm more noticeable now because I am 50," he said.

Maybe; maybe not.

The former Wake Forest graduate has posted five top-10 finishes and three top-five finishes in 20 previous Masters appearances.

His opening round included four birdies, three on the first nine, and one bogey at the 455-yard, par-4 fifth hole. He hit 12 of 18 greens in regulation and 10 of 14 fairways in his opening round but needed a mere 27 putts to negotiate the treacherous greens.

Can a 50-year-old win, Haas was asked, knowing that it has never happened here?

"I think anybody in the field can win, yes," he said, smiling.

"Is that a simple answer?"

Yes and no.

History tells us the oldest champion is Jack Nicklaus, who won the 1986 Tournament at 46 years, two months, and 23 days of age, the last of his six victories.

Jay Haas would like nothing better than to erase that record. ∎

Patrons enjoy a stroll on the grounds in the late afternoon sunshine.

Two-time champion Ben Crenshaw extricates himself from pine straw during the first round.

What They're Saying
(ROUND ONE)

It was a lot of mistakes and a lot of good things. There was just too much slack. But it was good for a while.

—*Two-time Masters champion Ben Crenshaw on his first-round 74*

He could make you laugh at the worst times and—I've said this many times—he's kicked me in the butt when I've needed to be kicked in the butt.

—*Former Masters champion Tom Watson, talking on the death of his longtime caddie and friend Bruce Edwards*

There's impending doom everywhere you go on the greens. You had to be conservative and that's probably part of being [my] first time here.

—*Shaun Micheel, a first-time Masters participant, on his impressions of Augusta National Golf Club*

LEADERS

HOLE	PRIOR	1	2	3	4	5	6	7	8	9	10	11	12	13	14	15	16	17	18
PAR		4	5	4	3	4	3	4	5	4	4	4	3	5	4	5	3	4	4
ROMERO	0	0	1	1	1	0	0	0	1	1	1	1	1	1	0				
FAXON	0	0	1	0	0	0	0	1	1	1	1	1	1	0	1	1	1		
PRICE P.	0	0	0	0	1	1	1	1	2	2	2	2	2	2	2				
LANGER	0	1	1	0	0	1	0	0	0	0	0	0	0	1	1	1	2	1	1
PRICE N.	0	0	1	1	0	0	0	1	1	1	1	1	1						
ROSE	0	1	2	2	2	2	2	2	2	3	3	2	2	3	3	3	3	4	5
ELS	0	0	1	1	1	1	1	1	2	2	2								
DiMARCO	0	0	0	0	0	2	2	2	2	2	2	2	2	2	2	3	3	3	
CLARKE	0	1	1	1	1	1	1	1	1	1	1	0	0	1	1	2	2	1	2
HAAS J.	0	1	2	2	2	1	1	2	2	2	2	2	2	3	3	3	3	3	3

THRU 10

O'MEARA	4
ELS	2
ALLENBY	1

Ernie Els scored a first round 70.

Round One LEADERS

Pos.	Player	Par	1	2	3	4	5	6	7	8	9	Out	10	11	12	13	14	15	16	17	18	In	Rd1	Total
		Par	4	5	4	3	4	3	4	5	4	36	4	4	3	5	4	5	3	4	4	36	72	
1	J. Rose	Score	3	4	4	3	4	3	4	5	3	33	4	5	3	4	4	5	3	3	3	34	67	−5
		Status	−1	−2	−2	−2	−2	−2	−2	−2	−3		−3	−2	−2	−3	−3	−3	−3	−4	−5			
T2	J. Haas	Score	3	4	4	3	5	3	3	5	4	34	4	4	3	4	4	5	3	4	4	35	69	−3
		Status	−1	−2	−2	−2	−1	−1	−2	−2	−2		−2	−2	−2	−3	−3	−3	−3	−3	−3			
T2	C. DiMarco	Score	4	5	4	3	4	1	4	5	4	34	4	4	3	5	4	4	3	4	4	35	69	−3
		Status	E	E	E	E	E	−2	−2	−2	−2		−2	−2	−2	−2	−2	−3	−3	−3	−3			
T4	C. Riley	Score	3	5	4	4	4	3	4	5	4	36	4	4	3	5	4	4	3	4	3	34	70	−2
		Status	−1	−1	−1	E	E	E	E	E	E		E	E	E	E	E	−1	−1	−1	−2			
T4	A. Cejka	Score	4	4	3	3	4	3	5	5	4	35	6	5	2	3	4	4	3	4	4	35	70	−2
		Status	E	−1	−2	−2	−2	−2	−1	−1	−1		+1	+2	+1	−1	−1	−2	−2	−2	−2			
T4	E. Els	Score	4	4	4	3	4	3	4	4	4	34	4	3	4	5	4	4	3	5	4	36	70	−2
		Status	E	−1	−1	−1	−1	−1	−1	−2	−2		−2	−3	−2	−2	−2	−3	−3	−2	−2			
T4	D. Clarke	Score	3	5	4	3	4	3	4	5	4	35	4	5	3	4	4	4	3	5	3	35	70	−2
		Status	−1	−1	−1	−1	−1	−1	−1	−1	−1		−1	E	E	−1	−1	−2	−2	−1	−2			

First-Round
SCORING

Rounds	93
Below 70	3
Below par	14
Par	7
Over par	72
80+	10
Scoring average	75.173
Low score	67
Justin Rose	
High score	88
Charles Coody	

First-Round Stat
LEADERS

Driving distance
D. Love III, 298.5 yards

Driving accuracy
S. Micheel, I. Poulter,
J. Rollins, G. Wolstenholme,
C. Stadler, N. Price, R. Floyd,
12 of 14

Greens in regulation
J. Rose, 17 of 18

Total putts
T. Watson, 24

Arnold Palmer acknowledged appreciative patrons with a wave of his putter.

Rose Remains in Full Bloom

III

While Arnold Palmer played his last competitive round at Augusta and received warm applause all day long, Justin Rose drew on his "hard" times as a professional to retain a two-stroke lead over former champion José Maria Olazabal and Alex Cejka.

He's 23 years old, hardly the age that qualifies someone as a wise old sage.

But at 23 Justin Rose has plenty of life experiences far beyond his years. He lost his father and golf teacher to leukemia in 2002. He suffered through 21 missed cuts in a row in a horrific first year as a professional, and he's learned to deal with pressures far greater than for most mature human beings.

All those things will help him, he said after retaining the lead at 36 holes with a one-under-par 71 and 138 total, two strokes better than Alex Cejka and two-time Masters champion José Maria Olazabal and three strokes better than Korea's K. J. Choi and Phil Mickelson.

"In a lot of ways, you have experiences that make you realize that it's not the end of the world, and other experiences that make you tougher," Rose said.

After two rounds, Rose will have to call upon all those experiences to be in a position to win his first major championship.

With 44 players surviving the cut and 12 within five shots of Rose's lead, the pressure will be staggering as the final two rounds unfold.

That doesn't seem to faze Rose, however.

"I feel like I can draw on a couple of things that have happened to me going into the weekend," the Englishman said after a sunny day saw the field struggle to make more precise iron shots count and to work extremely hard for whatever birdies came their way.

Only seven sub-70 rounds were record by the field. Davis Love III and left-hander Steve Flesch shot the low rounds of the day, with five-under-par 67s.

There were, however, more train wrecks than success stories after the midway point of the Tournament.

Choi, for example, was seven under par after nine holes and made four bogeys on the second nine to negate his record-tying 30 going out. It was a 70, but . . .

"As I got going, I kept making birdies," said the 33-year-old from Wando, Korea.

Was he disappointed in a four-over-par 40 coming in? Choi was asked.

On Friday, Arnold Palmer strikes his final competitive tee shot at the first hole at the Masters.

When his final Masters Tournament was complete, Arnold Palmer shared an emotional moment with his granddaughter by the 18th green.

"I thought even par would be a good score, but finishing at two under par I feel very lucky."

Others weren't so lucky on a day when Arnold Palmer played in his record 50th and final Masters.

Thirteen missed the cut score of four-over-par 148 by a single stroke.

A handful of them fell victim to nerves at the 465-yard, par-4 18th hole. Former champion Larry Mize triple-bogeyed the hole and missed the cut by two strokes. Former champions Ray Floyd, Craig Stadler, and Mike Weir bogeyed the hole to miss by a stroke. John Daly, Robert Allenby, and Michael Campbell, all proven tournament winners, also bogeyed the final hole to miss by a single stroke.

Other casualties of the cut included two-time champion Ben Crenshaw (74–75), six-time champion Jack Nicklaus (75–75), and three-time champion Nick Faldo (76–75).

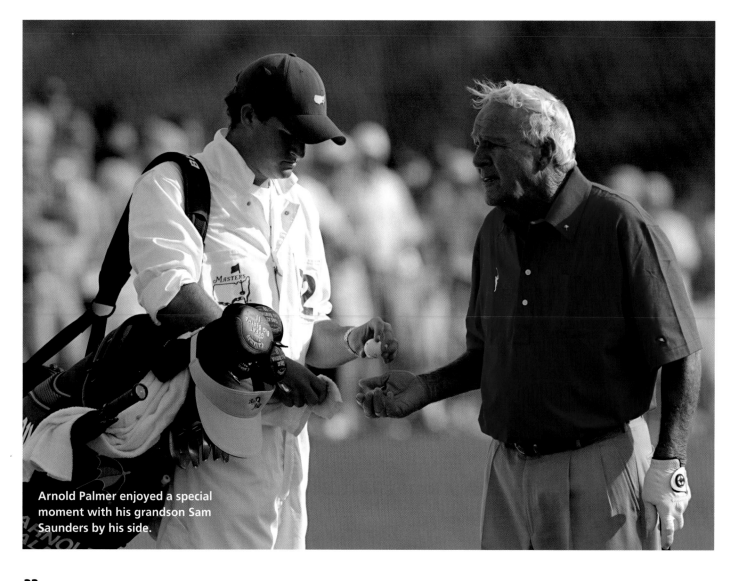

Arnold Palmer enjoyed a special moment with his grandson Sam Saunders by his side.

Augusta National was a cruel mistress in the second round, said many in the field.

"The golf course is not getting softer," said Augusta native Charles Howell III following a second 71 and 142 total that tied him for sixth.

"Anybody in the red [under par] has a chance on the weekend," said 1998 champion Mark O'Meara.

Jeff Sluman believes O'Meara is right after shooting rounds of 73–70–143, five behind Rose.

"I'll see how the golf course is set up and where the pins are," he said after a warm, sunny day, "and if the weather stays like this it will be tough this weekend."

The stern test just tortures you, said veteran Kirk Triplett, who shot 74 and totaled 145. "I would have loved to be under par. I just got worn out. That is what this course is. It is a mental and physical challenge."

Rose seemed impervious to the pressure around him.

He'll tell you that trying to make a cut was much tougher.

"There were times when I thought this [career] is taking a long time to sort itself out," he said after a steady two-birdie, one-bogey round.

Shot of the Day
(ROUND TWO)

José Maria Olazabal feels extremely comfortable at Augusta National Golf Club, and on no hole does he feel more comfortable than on the 510-yard, par-5 13th hole, a hole requiring a right-to-left tee shot and the courage to boldly strike a second shot over water. Olazabal's courage in the second round provided an eagle three at the hole, the third of his career. He hit a driver and a 3-iron to 36 feet and sank the putt. It took the two-time champion from one under par to three under par. Olazabal has now eagled No. 13 more than he has any other par-5. He finished with 69 and a 36-hole total of 140, two strokes behind leader Justin Rose.

Justin Rose follows his tee shot at the par-5 15th hole.

Patrons provided an impressive panorama of numbers and colors as Arnold Palmer plays hole No. 18 in his final competitive round in the Masters.

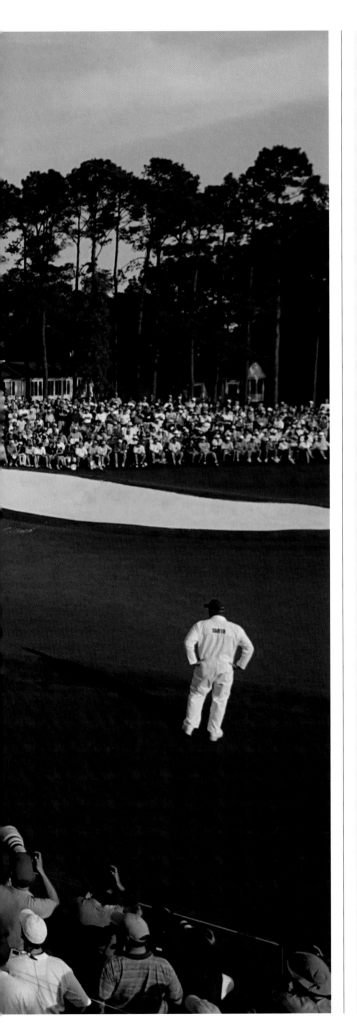

What They're Writing
(ROUND TWO)

It is a story etched in Masters folklore, how Gary Player took José Maria Olazabal aside one time and gave him a pep talk. Told the Spaniard to play with confidence, to believe in himself.

And this year? Did Player pull him aside again?

"Yeah," said Olazabal. "I think he's really tired of telling me the same thing."

Player's impatience would be understandable. Olazabal, a gifted shot-maker and unmatched competitor, has on countless occasions gone into such a funk with his swing that the periods of bad play are tough to imagine for such a standout.

—Jim McCabe, Boston Globe

On a glorious day in a glorious place, perhaps the most influential man in golf made his final trip around one of the most special places in the game.

Arnold Palmer's 50th and final Masters came to a close in the most perfect of conditions, other than, of course, the fact that he shot a pair of matching 84s. Numbers, however, had little to do with this day. It was about family, friends, tradition, and a place and tournament that Palmer truly loves.

—Mike Dudurich, Pittsburgh Tribune Review

There was a period in the late 1950s and early '60s when thousands of weekend duffers tried to emulate Arnold Palmer's slap shot of a golf swing. Chiropractors still refer to it as The Golden Age.

But many more spines were tingled by Palmer than put out of alignment, and that crazy, wonderful swing ended up democratizing a sport that had been cooped up in country clubs. It made golf dashing for the masses in the way James Bond made espionage dashing.

—Rick Morrissey, Chicago Tribune

A wink, a hug, a wave to the crowd. Without even swinging a club, Arnold Palmer has always known how to make the people smile.

The King did it again Friday, closing out his competitive career at the Masters during one last sentimental stroll around Augusta National, the course he carried straight into American culture over the past 50 years.

"It's not fun sometimes to know it's over," he said afterward, fighting through the tears.

—Doug Ferguson, Associated Press

He said he had coped with it because he knew how awful it was to feel the wrong kind of pressure at the wrong end of the game.

He said he could deal with the pressure of leading the U.S. Masters for a second day in succession because he knew what it was like to miss 21 cuts in a row.

Besides that, he said, trying to hang on to the dream of winning the greatest prize in golf was easy.

"This is fun," Justin Rose said.

—Oliver Holt, London Mirror

HOLE NO. 18

Name: Holly

Par 4; 465 yards

One of the most famous finishing holes in golf, this uphill dogleg right has taken the measure of many a golfer, and nowhere was that more evident than in the second round. A total of 13 players missed the 36-hole cut by one stroke, and the finishing hole played a cruel part in that. Former champions Craig Stadler, MIke Weir, and Ray Floyd bogeyed the final hole to miss by one stroke. Former champion Larry Mize triple-bogeyed the hole to miss by two strokes. Craig Perks (double bogey), Robert Allenby (bogey), Michael Campbell (bogey), and John Daley (bogey) also missed playing on the weekend by a single shot.

The beautiful and challenging final hole of Augusta National.

"I felt like every time I was in 'contention' to make the cut, I felt like there was an incredible amount of pressure on me. It seemed at the time that cameras would appear from the trees and suddenly, 'Justin has a chance to make the cut for the first time.' That was just the way I saw it, which was probably completely the wrong way to see it. I'm trying to deal with that."

Rose said he put an inordinate amount of pressure on himself in those days "and when I finally did [make a cut] it was like winning a tournament.

"And winning four times," he said of his worldwide career record since he stepped over that hurdle, "obviously believing that you can win under pressure, that will help as well."

Those behind him also have pressure in different ways.

A study in concentration, Vijay Singh focuses on this putt during his round.

In the special moment, four-time winner Arnold Palmer walks across the Byron Nelson Bridge at the 13th hole for the last time in the Tournament.

Arnold Palmer

(ROUND TWO)

Like all good military units, they stood stiffly at attention when their general arrived to take center stage.

After all, Arnie's Army was born here in about 1958, and so fittingly it would take its last stand here, too, in the gentle and sylvan Georgia countryside.

During his sojourn, patrons clapped so enthusiastically that their hands ached with love for Arnold Palmer during the second round of the Masters. It began at the first tee and ended with the characteristic and familiar wave of the hand from the man of the hour.

Saying good-bye is never easy. Saying good-bye to a hero is twice as hard. You don't want to let go of those who seem bigger than life.

But patrons did it with relish for Palmer, who completed a record-setting 50 Masters with the same style and grace he led his life—in a first-class manner.

The tribute and adulation touched Palmer, who had his grandson Sam Saunders by his side through-out his farewell as his caddie. His daughters and grandchildren, as well as his fiancée, Kit Gawthorp, were on hand for the touching tribute.

"Augusta and this golf tournament have been about a part of my life as anything other than my family," said the 74-year-old four-time Masters champion. "I don't think that I could ever separate myself from this Club and this golf tournament. I may not be present, I may not be here, but I'll still be part of what happens here only because I want to be."

Palmer said he will still come to the Champions dinner.

Yet, said Palmer, his Masters career is done.

"It's time for me for it to be done," he said resignedly. "I won't say I'm happy it's done."

The memories, however, will last forever, he said.

"I can never tell you how important these fans and the media were to me," he said afterward.

Yes, Palmer said, he thought about how many times he walked up the 18th fairway with a Green Jacket awaiting him at the other end.

Yes, Palmer said, he thought about that first Masters in 1955 and all the wonderful years in between.

"Emotion," he said. "There was a lot."

"One of the things I wanted to do I did today—I finished 50 years of golf at the Masters."

And so he did.

Using his familiar thumbs-up gesture, Arnold Palmer greets patrons.

Cejka, who escaped from Communist Czechoslovakia at age nine, is a four-time winner on the European Tour, but has not played in the Masters since 1996, his only appearance.

Maturity will help him, he said, after a five-birdie, three-bogey day.

"The game has improved a little bit I think mentally, especially. I've got more experience; '96 was the first tournament in America, first major. I was young. I was wild," he said.

But not quite as wild anymore, said the 34-year-old.

Olazabal, now 38 and five years removed since his second and last major victory, wonders whether the changes to Augusta National can compliment his title chances.

"I don't know if it fits my game," said Olazabal of the layout.

He does, however, love the ambience of the grounds.

"The years are going by, the golf course is changing a lot. Changes have been huge since '99." However, he added, "It's a great point in favor of the player that knows the course really well."

Count Olazabal among those with an intimate knowledge of the storied layout, a short game second to none, and enough length to keep him in contention.

The second round was a keen example of enough length to keep Olazabal interested in the chase.

He hit a driver and a 3-iron to 36 feet on the par-5 13th and holed the putt for an

His straw hat filled with a treasure trove of past Masters badges, a long time patron watches second round play.

What They're Saying
(ROUND TWO)

Augusta is the only place where you can chip and still not keep it on the green. This is a funny place.

—*Augusta native Charles Howell III on the difficulty of the course*

Anytime you get to the weekend here, you are going to be right there. You are going to have a chance for a very nice finish.

—*Kirk Triplett after a 74 left him at one over par for the Tournament*

The golf course when you're not playing well eats you up. And then you're playing defensively and that's not what you want to do out here.

—*1976 Masters champion Ray Floyd on the difficulty of poor play at Augusta National*

I think this is the first time I ever shot 30 on a front nine in nine holes. The fact that it came today at the Masters, I feel very lucky that it did."

—*Korea's K. J. Choi on his record-tying first-nine score during the second round*

I've got a lot of great memories here. I've shot scores that can win, so I've just got to keep after it.

—*Georgia resident Davis Love III on his quest for a Masters Tournament win*

Despite an unconventional grip, Chris DiMarco was deadly accurate with his putting, as was the case on the second green.

eagle, made a 15-footer for birdie on the par-4 14th, then chipped to within a foot at par-5 15 for another birdie to highlight his round.

The aura of the Masters keeps gnawing at his competitive psyche, said Olazabal.

"It must be something with this place," he said, unable to put his finger exactly on the reason. "Every time I come here, I try to do my best. I feel in a way a little bit at peace with myself."

With 44 players remaining in the hunt, what will the final 36 holes bring?

Four of the top five players are International players. From 1988 to 1996, seven International players won Masters titles in a nine-year period.

Can that trend begin again?

Bernhard Langer kept his eyes squarely on his second shot to the first green.

Alex Cejka
(ROUND TWO)

Sometimes golfers have a tendency to take things for granted.

After all, their lifestyle takes them to exotic places, and people treat them well.

Complacency like that will never happen to Alex Cejka.

And it will never, ever happen at the Masters.

Cejka appreciates places such as Augusta National Golf Club, just as he appreciates the sacrifices his father made many years ago to remove him from Communist rule in Czechoslovakia.

Cejka posted his second-straight 70 over the 7,290-yard, par-72 course, leaving him four under par and within two shots of the 36-hole lead.

Like many International players, Cejka came to the United States with a desire to face the best players on the best courses.

He reveled in his return to the Masters after an eight-year absence.

Now 34, he realizes he was too young in 1996, when he placed 44th.

"The game has improved a little bit, I think mentally, especially," he said of his skills.

"I've got more experience; '96 was the first tournament in America, first major. I was young. I was wild. So it was a great experience for me."

Cejka has won four times on the PGA European Tour, including three times in 1995, his breakthrough year.

But golf pales in comparison to his escape from Czechoslovakia at age nine.

"It's been quite a while," said Cejka of the trip with his father, also named Alex.

"I was actually too young to understand what was going on. I was on holiday with my father and he just took me on a trip."

At dusk one night in 1980 the elder Cejka took his son to a river along the border, and they swam to freedom.

Given his young age, he can't remember the name or where the escape to freedom actually took place.

"I didn't know the risks," he said. "I didn't know what could happen if they catch us. But it turned out very good. We did it. I'm very proud of my dad that he made this decision and tried to do it instead of staying in communism."

Nearly a quarter century later—and after a lifetime learning the game in Germany—Cejka is more concentrated on a high Masters finish.

He knows he's a more complete player these days and wants to show it.

"I had a good preparation," he said of his run-up to the event.

"I was here on the weekend already. I played the course a few times. I played every wind. I played in the morning, in the afternoon. I was ready. My game is ready. I've been playing well."

Now, he said, it's time to show the world.

Lian-Wei Zhang studies the nuances of Augusta National Golf Club greens in his first Masters appearance.

Did You Know?

(ROUND TWO)

At age 74, Arnold Palmer was the fourth-oldest player to make a start at the Masters. The oldest was Fred McLeod at age 79 in 1962, and both Jock Hutchison and Doug Ford competed at age 77.

Gary Player made his 47th Masters start and at age 68 is the oldest International player to start in the Masters.

In the history of the event, three players—Lloyd Mangrum (1940), Tony Lema (1963), and Dan Pohl (1982)—finished second in their first Masters but never improved on that. Mangrum played in 20 Masters, while Lema and Pohl played in four and seven, respectively.

When Korea's K. J. Choi shot a first-nine 30 during the second round, he tied a record held by Johnny Miller (third round, 1975) and Greg Norman (fourth round, 1988).

Since a 36-hole cut was instituted in 1957, Jack Nicklaus—as you might expect—tops all players in playing the final two rounds. Prior to the 2004 event, Nicklaus had made the midway cut in 37 of his 43 Masters Tournaments.

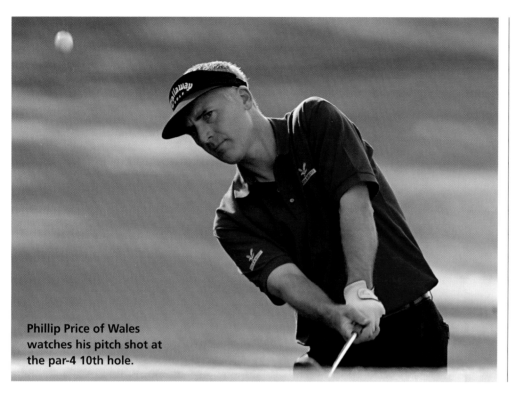

Phillip Price of Wales watches his pitch shot at the par-4 10th hole.

Or will someone like the supremely talented Mickelson, thwarted in majors during his career, become the second left-handed player in a row to win the Masters? Mickelson, playing the best golf of his career, starts the third round only three strokes off the lead.

Could Mickelson break his so-called major jinx in 2004?

If those answers unfold in usual Masters style, they will be surprising, scintillating, and dramatic to be sure.

Or at least it always seems to be that way. ∎

Second-Round SCORING

Rounds	93
Below 70	7
Below par	22
Par	11
Over par	60
80+	6
Scoring average	73.784
Low score	67
Davis Love III, Steve Flesch	
High score	84
Arnold Palmer	

Second-Round Stat LEADERS

Driving distance
F. Couples, 299.0 yards

Driving accuracy
T. Clark, F. Funk, 14 of 14

Greens in regulation
I. Poulter, 17 of 18

Total putts
D. Love III, 23

With his characteristic full body turn, Sergio Garcia registered a second even par 72 in his round.

Watched by patrons, Arnold Palmer strikes a fairway wood.

Round Two
LEADERS

Pos.	Player	Par	1	2	3	4	5	6	7	8	9	Out	10	11	12	13	14	15	16	17	18	In	Rd2	Total
			4	5	4	3	4	3	4	5	4	36	4	4	3	5	4	5	3	4	4	36	72	
1	**J. Rose**	Score	4	5	4	3	3	3	4	5	4	35	4	5	2	5	4	5	3	4	4	36	71	138
		Status	−5	−5	−5	−5	−6	−6	−6	−6	−6		−6	−5	−6	−6	−6	−6	−6	−6	−6			
T2	**J. Olazabal**	Score	4	5	3	3	4	4	4	5	4	36	4	4	3	3	3	4	3	4	5	33	69	140
		Status	−1	−1	−2	−2	−2	−1	−1	−1	−1		−1	−1	−1	−3	−4	−5	−5	−5	−4			
T2	**A. Cejka**	Score	4	4	4	3	3	2	5	5	4	34	4	4	4	4	4	5	3	3	5	36	70	140
		Status	−2	−3	−3	−3	−4	−5	−4	−4	−4		−4	−4	−3	−4	−4	−4	−4	−5	−4			
T4	**K. J. Choi**	Score	4	4	3	3	3	3	3	4	3	30	5	5	4	5	4	5	4	4	4	40	70	141
		Status	−1	−2	−3	−3	−4	−4	−5	−6	−7		−6	−5	−4	−4	−4	−4	−3	−3	−3			
T4	**P. Mickelson**	Score	4	5	3	4	4	3	4	5	4	36	4	4	2	4	4	5	3	3	4	33	69	141
		Status	E	E	−1	E	E	E	E	E	E		E	E	−1	−2	−2	−2	−2	−3	−3			

Two College Friends Dream of Green Jacket

Phil Mickelson and Chris DiMarco share the 54-hole lead while four International players, including two-time Masters winner Bernhard Langer and three-time major winner Ernie Els, are in close pursuit.

On a day when only 13 subpar rounds were in order, two old college friends and rivals found themselves dreaming of a date with a Green Jacket.

Phil Mickelson, a supremely talented player with a string of near misses in the majors, and Chris DiMarco, himself an 18- and 36-hole leader of the Masters in 2001, moved closer to golf immortality after three rounds.

The two friends shared the 54-hole lead and expect to share a final round of thrust and parry with 42 other players for the right to be called the 2004 Masters champion.

"I think that Chris and I really enjoy playing together," said Mickelson, a former rival of DiMarco's when the former was at Arizona State University and the latter at the University of Florida.

"We're going to have a fun day. We played together a bunch in college. It's weird that we used to compete in collegiate tournaments and here we are competing Sunday at Augusta in the final group."

"I've known Phil since college," said DiMarco. "I guess I was a junior when he was a freshman. So we've played a lot of tournaments together."

The two also teamed with each other in the Presidents Cup last winter in George, South Africa.

Both know there's much more at stake than collegiate bragging rights, much more. The Masters is a Grand Slam event that can make careers. Neither has won such an event in his life, and many believed Mickelson would have done so by age 33.

He has a string of near misses in the U.S. Open and the PGA Championship, where he's finished second.

DiMarco hasn't had that success yet. He shot a third-round 68 under sunny skies and warm temperatures. Mickelson shot 69.

Their aggregate scores of 6-under-par 210 left them two shots clear of Englishman Paul Casey, who shot 68, and three clear of two-time Masters winner Bernhard Langer (69), Ernie Els (71), and K. J. Choi (72) at 213.

Kirk Triplett's 69 put him at 214 and in seventh place, and Sweden's Fredrik

Surrounded by patrons, Phil Mickelson used all his short-game skills on this shot to the final green.

With the scoreboard in the background, leader Justin Rose plays a short iron to the third green.

Jacobson's 67—the best round of the day—gave him an aggregate of 215, one under par.

Only eight players were under par, 215 or better.

England's Justin Rose, the 36-hole leader, struggled through a string of early bogeys

and shot 81. He was at 219 and tied for 20th place.

With Sunday at Augusta looming, no one could be ruled out of the picture.

But Mickelson and DiMarco seemed in the driver's seat.

Mickelson managed to card three

birdies and no bogeys in his round. He has found better control of his driver this year, and playing from the fairways has given him an advantage heretofore unknown to him.

"I think the decision-making has improved for the simple reason I've been driving the ball in play," said Mickelson, who ranks first in scoring on the PGA Tour. "I don't have the decisions that I had when I was off in the trees as much. It's a much easier game, driving it in play, and even when I do miss a fairway, it's by a small amount rather than big misses."

What They're Saying
(ROUND THREE)

I am still a bit shell-shocked, to be honest. Whether you believe me or not, I felt in a great frame of mind going out there. I hit the ball beautifully on the range.

> —*Midway leader Justin Rose after shooting 81 and totaling 219, nine shots behind the coleaders*

This course is perfect for him. He's long and has great imagination around the greens.

> —*Georgian Stewart Cink on Phil Mickelson's chances to win the Masters*

Saturday at a major, if you don't have it all, it will get you pretty quick.

> —*Amateur Brandt Snedeker on his 3-over-par 75 third-round score in his first Masters*

I think it's good. People have their place. Why make them move?

> —*Retief Goosen speaking about the new play-off format that begins at No. 18 instead of No. 10*

Sergio Garcia, facing page, K. J. Choi, Chris DiMarco, and Davis Love III, clockwise from left, all found themselves in a bunker in front of the second green.

What They're Writing

(ROUND THREE)

With a revamped, tighter swing that has provided more accuracy off the tee, better distance control and less anxiety, a slimmed-down Phil Mickelson admitted Saturday he has been playing the best golf of his life this year.

But Mickelson had even more reason for joy after the third round of the Masters. And it wasn't because a three-under-par 69 gave him the 54-hole lead in a major for the first time. Or that he was tied with former college buddy/foe and Presidents Cup partner Chris DiMarco, who also shot one of the three bogey-free rounds (68) for a 6-under 210 total.

No, Mickelson's biggest delight was in major nemesis Tiger Woods being nine shots back in a tie for 20th after a second 75 this week at Augusta National.

—Bruce Berlet, Hartford Courant

He's where he's never been before. Twelve years as a professional, 12 years of botched drives or yanked putts, 12 years of being asked why he couldn't scale the mountain, and Phil Mickelson never had led or shared the lead of a major golf tournament going into the final day, much less won a major golf tournament.

But he's there now. He's tied for first in the Masters with his pal Chris DiMarco.

He's where he's never been before, but the only issue is where he'll be tonight. Free at last of the label as "the best player without a major victory" or tortured once more by another near-miss?

—Art Spander, Oakland Tribune

On Sunday at the Masters, where he [Mickelson] is tied for the lead, we'll see if that fundamental change [no longer attempting risky shots], one that has always run to the very core of his personality, finally makes the difference.

We'll see, after so many New Phil approaches and fresh mind-sets, if abandoning the thrill of chance was the true cure to his diabolical personal puzzle. We'll see if the prodigiously gifted man who is 0 for 46 in major championships achieves his long-sought triumph in a Big One.

—Tom Boswell, Washington Post

In 54 holes, Mickelson has hit 31 of 42 fairways (73.8 percent) and 41 of 54 greens in regulation (75.9 percent). He hit 10 of 14 fairways in the third round, and that enabled him to hit 12 of 18 greens. He needed only 27 putts.

Mickelson's confidence in his game—he's already won this year on the PGA Tour—has left him at peace with his quest for a major championship.

"I think that heading into the final round I'm much more at ease than I have been in the past, where I've been anxious and wondering how it is going to go on the range beforehand, or am I going to drive it in play or is my swing going to be there," he said of past demons.

Mickelson will tell you near misses have made the continued chase a fun challenge.

"I've really enjoyed the challenge of trying to break through because it has been so difficult," said the Californian. "Things are more rewarding when they are difficult."

DiMarco, a three-time winner on the PGA Tour since turning pro in 1990, also seeks the elusive major title on his résumé.

He believes he's more prepared for the stress that comes with being in the final pairing on the final day in the Masters.

Phil Mickelson's club selection was accurate all week.

Davis Love III watches as his tee
shot heads toward the 12th green.

Surrounded by patrons and in a sylvan setting, the 16th hole is a popular viewing spot.

"I'm a lot more prepared," he said after a third round that provided four birdies and no bogeys. "I think the Presidents Cup really helped me last year. I think that under that kind of pressure and to be able to perform really lifted me; [I] felt like it brought my game to a new level."

DiMarco said being in the Presidents Cup pressure cooker and knowing the U.S. team needed him to defeat Stuart Appleby to keep the Americans in the match was important.

DiMarco did pull off that victory, with a birdie on the 17th hole for a one-up decision. The U.S. and the International Teams eventually played to a tie.

Shot of the Day
(ROUND THREE)

A thrill for any player at the Masters is winning crystal, which is given for everything from the day's low score to a hole-in-one to an eagle or a double eagle.

Amateur Casey Wittenberg of Memphis, Tennessee, will take home more than memories. He's taking home a pair of engraved Masters crystal goblets after making an eagle two at the downhill and enticing 495-yard, par-4 10th hole.

Wittenberg holed out a 177 yard, 7-iron for the deuce.

"I heard the crowd's reaction and I knew it was either close or went in," said the 19-year-old Oklahoma State University golfer.

"It was unbelievable that it was on that hole and in this tournament." Wittenberg, playing in his first Masters, shot 71 and was at 219.

"To be able to do that with that much intensity flowing through me, that's probably what I've learned most," he said. "I obviously want to win majors, certainly. I want to win more tournaments. But if it all ended tomorrow, I'd be happy with my career the way I've played and what I've done and the success I've had."

Yet just because the two ended the third round as coleaders doesn't mean they will be able to claim the Masters title.

The other players and the golf course will have much to say about it, as usual.

A fast start and timely putting might allow someone behind Mickelson and DiMarco to shoot a low number and pass them.

Holding the lead at the Masters is also akin to being in a pressure cooker that's ready to pop its lid.

The latter factor, you would think, might rule out someone like Casey, a first-time participant, but don't bet on it, said Mickelson.

"Well, there's not going to be any match play because we've got a number of guys that will [chase us]," said the man known for his superb short game and golden putting stroke.

"Paul Casey at four under and a number

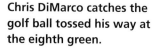

Chris DiMarco catches the golf ball tossed his way at the eighth green.

Patrons in observation stands get a panoramic view of the 11th green, left, and the 12th hole and the 13th tee.

Alex Cejka of Germany watches as his putt on the third green heads toward the hole.

HOLE NO. 11

Name: White Dogwood

Par 4; 490 yards

In 2002 the tee on this hole was lengthened 30 to 35 yards and moved five yards to the right. Prior to the 2004 Masters, 36 pine trees—some as tall as 35 feet—were added to the right of the fairway, requiring a more precise tee shot and a longer, downhill second shot to a green guarded by a pond at the front left and a bunker behind the green. In the third round, the difficulty of the hole was apparent. It played to 4.523 strokes, yielding only a birdie to two-time Masters champion Bernhard Langer. There were 13 bogeys, including by 36-hole leader Justin Rose; four double bogeys; and a triple bogey, by Jeff Sluman.

Did You Know?

Over the course of the previous 14 Masters Tournaments, the eventual winner has come from the final pairing. Tiger Woods has won three times in the final pairing. José Maria Olazabal has won twice from the last group.

—

Of the three players at the top of the leader board searching for their first major championship, Phil Mickelson has had the most chances (46). Four of those came as an amateur. Chris DiMarco has had 17 chances and Paul Casey just five.

—

In the previous 67 Masters Tournaments, 37 players who either held or shared the third-round lead have gone on to victory, including six of the last 10. Tiger Woods was the last to accomplish that feat, in 2002.

—

Swede Fredrik Jacobson made the biggest move up the scoreboard in the third round. After making the cut at 148, Jacobson shot 67 and jumped from a T32 to a T8. There were 13 sub-par rounds from the 44 players in the third round.

—

There were three bogey-free third rounds, by Stewart Cink (69), Chris DiMarco (68), and Phil Mickelson (69).

Davis Love III faced a delicate third shot to the seventh green during his round.

Paul Casey strokes a
putt toward the cup.

Paul Casey

(ROUND THREE)

There has been nothing "rookie" about first-time Masters participant Paul Casey's play through three rounds of the Masters.

He added a third-round four-under-par 68 to rounds of 75 and 69 for a 54-hole total of 212, two strokes behind coleaders Phil Mickelson and Chris DiMarco.

Casey hit 13 of 18 greens in regulation but only nine of 14 fairways on the day. He needed 27 putts, his lowest putting total by five in each of the two previous rounds.

Casey, a three-time winner on the PGA European Tour, has relaxed and allowed himself to forget the pressures of chasing a major championship this week.

"I think I've just approached this differently to how I've approached majors in the past," he said. "I think I've put too much pressure on myself in the past, and these are the events we're trying to win out here, that every professional golfer would dearly love to win. I've almost tried too hard."

In five Grand Slam appearances prior to the Masters, Casey's best finish is 66th, in the 2003 PGA Championship.

He came to the Masters with a top-10 finish at the Players Championship a few weeks earlier.

Mickelson said to watch out for the former Arizona State University player.

"Paul and I have been good friends for quite some time," said Mickelson, also a former ASU golfer.

"I think Paul Casey is one of the best players in the world. He's a guy who hits the ball a long way, has great irons, a good putter. I put him, and always have put him, in the likes of Adam Scotts and Justin Roses, the good solid young players to keep an eye out for."

Five birdies and one bogey resulted in the third-round 68 and left Casey dreaming of being the next United Kingdom player to don a Green Jacket.

"Being a Masters champion strikes a nerve back in the U.K., because of the success the Europeans have had," he said, mentioning past champions Sandy Lyle, Ian Woosnam, Nick Faldo, José Maria Olazabal, and Seve Ballesteros.

"I would dearly love to continue that trend. The [British] Open Championship is the one I would love to win. I mean, it's our national championship. But this is a very, very close second. You know I'd love to be putting on that Green Jacket and be up in that special locker room upstairs."

Maybe he will yet.

Keeping his eye on the players below him, a forecaddie watches for approach shots to the 10th green.

of guys at three [are] only a couple of shots back. I think Paul Casey is one of the best players in the world."

Mickelson and Casey are both products of Arizona State University, albeit in different eras.

Casey's third-round scorecard was dotted with five birdies and one bogey.

The 26-year-old is a fourth-year pro with boyish good looks and charm to match.

With no success in five previous Grand Slam events, Casey took a different tack for the Masters. He took pressure off himself.

"I think I've put too much pressure on myself in the past," he said of two appearances in the British Open Championship and the PGA Championship and one in the U.S. Open, where his best finish is 66th and includes four missed cuts.

"I've almost tried too hard and I think

since this whole year, I've been very relaxed and approached things the correct way."

Casey will tell you that approach was necessary because he felt he was shooting scores but "the scores weren't matching the effort level."

History, however, is against his victory on Easter Sunday.

In the long and glorious history of the Masters only three players have ever won in their first appearance.

Those include Horton Smith in 1934 (the inaugural year of the Masters), Gene Sarazen in 1935, and Fuzzy Zoeller in 1979.

Negating all that, it's always impossible to tell what will transpire in the final round.

Augusta National Golf Club, after all, identifies and crowns only the most worthy of champions.

It should be no different in 2004. ∎

Round Three LEADERS

Pos.	Player	Par	1	2	3	4	5	6	7	8	9	Out	10	11	12	13	14	15	16	17	18	In	Rd3	Total
			4	5	4	3	4	3	4	5	4	36	4	4	3	5	4	5	3	4	4	36	72	
T1	C. DiMarco	Score	4	4	4	2	4	3	4	4	4	33	4	4	3	5	3	5	3	4	4	35	68	210
		Status	−2	−3	−3	−4	−4	−4	−4	−5	−5		−5	−5	−5	−5	−6	−6	−6	−6	−6			
T1	P. Mickelson	Score	4	5	3	3	4	3	3	4	4	33	4	4	3	5	4	5	3	4	4	36	69	210
		Status	−3	−3	−4	−4	−4	−4	−5	−6	−6		−6	−6	−6	−6	−6	−6	−6	−6	−6			
3	P. Casey	Score	4	5	3	3	3	4	3	5	3	33	4	4	3	5	4	4	3	4	4	35	68	212
		Status	E	E	−1	−1	−2	−1	−2	−2	−3		−3	−3	−3	−3	−3	−4	−4	−4	−4			
T4	K. J. Choi	Score	4	5	5	3	4	3	4	5	3	36	4	5	3	4	4	5	3	4	4	36	72	213
		Status	−3	−3	−2	−2	−2	−2	−2	−2	−3		−3	−2	−2	−3	−3	−3	−3	−3	−3			
T4	B. Langer	Score	4	4	4	3	5	3	4	5	3	35	4	3	3	5	5	3	3	4	4	34	69	213
		Status	E	−1	−1	−1	E	E	E	E	−1		−1	−2	−2	−2	−1	−3	−3	−3	−3			
T4	E. Els	Score	4	4	4	3	3	3	4	5	4	34	4	5	4	3	6	4	4	3	4	37	71	213
		Status	−2	−3	−3	−3	−4	−4	−4	−4	−4		−4	−3	−3	−2	−2	−3	−3	−3	−3			

Fantastic Phil Finish

Phil Mickelson won the Masters, and his first major title, with a clinching birdie on the 72nd hole—one of only four players ever to do so. The dramatic putt ended one of the most exciting Tournaments, with a one-stroke win over Ernie Els.

When his defining career moment came on a cloudy April day, Phil Mickelson jumped spread-eagle into the Georgia air in ecstasy.

When the 18-foot birdie putt curled halfway around the cup and fell in, Mickelson joined an exclusive and long-coveted club—a Masters champion.

He gave the patrons a thumbs-up gesture and flashed a smile as wide as his face would allow, showing those pearly white teeth to their maximum.

He hugged his wife, Amy, and squeezed each of his three kids with the joy only a major championship can bring.

Mickelson's long and sometimes frustrating winless streak in major tournaments ended. Forever. Boy, did that 43 long Green Jacket feel good.

Instead of being the victim this time, Mickelson was the victimizer, beating South African Ernie Els by a shot with birdies on two of the last three holes.

Mickelson shot a final round 69 and nine-under-par total of 279. Els' final round of 67, which included holding the lead until the last-minute heroics, added up to 280, marking his second runner-up finish and sixth top-10 Masters finish, five in a row.

"I played as good as I could," said three-time major championship winner Els disappointedly. "I guess Phil deserved this one."

K. J. Choi was third, with a final round of 69 and 282. Sergio Garcia played a 12-hole stretch in seven under par for a 66, and two-time Masters champion Bernhard Langer, who held a share of the lead during the round but shot 72, tied for fourth at three-under-par. A total of 18 of 44 players broke par Sunday over the 7,290-yard, par-72 layout.

On a day in which two holes-in-one were recorded—by Padraig Harrington and Kirk Triplett at the par-3 16th hole in successive pairings—and when eagles flew into the hole seemingly at every turn, Mickelson took a big burden off his back.

The highly talented Rancho Santa Fe, California, resident had gone 46 majors without a victory, leaving him long overdue to step up to the next professional level.

Phil Mickelson watches as his wedge shot heads to the second green.

His maturity—some see it as an inner peace—and a better control of his driving and short game paid big dividends at Augusta National.

And he relished the feeling more than he could ever explain.

"I think I yelled out, 'I did it!'" he said. "I think that's what I yelled out. It was a little surreal. I couldn't believe it finally happened. It's hard to explain how it feels. It feels almost make-believe."

Mickelson observers—some in his coterie of confidants and friends and some not—believe a different player emerged following a winless and disappointing 2003 PGA Tour season.

Mickelson rededicated himself to improving both his driving accuracy and

Chris DiMarco's 5-iron shot found the left edge of the putting surface at the fourth hole, but he three-putted for a bogey.

What They're Saying
(ROUND FOUR)

I just feel like I played well enough to win. Unfortunately, I'm just not going to. That's the majors.

> —*Spaniard Sergio Garcia after shooting 66*

It was a good week, a great experience, a great time. I learned a lot and know what it takes to play out here.

> —*Amateur Brandt Snedeker, who tied for 41st place*

I just got momentum and that is what you need.

> —*Australian Stephen Leaney after playing the last eight holes in six under par*

I didn't make any putts this week. You can't go around here and not putt well and expect to win.

> —*Three-time champion Tiger Woods, who shot 2-over-par 290 for the second straight year*

It was a spectacular week to have my dad on the bag and do this.

> —*Casey Wittenberg, who shot even-par 288 and was low amateur*

Bernhard Langer studies a key putt at the 18th green before tying for fourth.

his short game, specifically his distance control with the irons. He lost some weight in an effort to make his golf changes work also.

"I'm so happy for him," said Mickelson's teacher Rick Smith. "He's done the work and it shows through the results."

Smith and short-game instructor Dave Pelz worked with Mickelson in the off-season to sharpen his skills, and the sessions paid off handsomely. He had already won on the PGA Tour prior to the Masters and had posted seven top-10 finishes in eight events.

Mickelson began the final round sharing the 54-hole lead with former collegiate rival Chris DiMarco.

DiMarco, burdened with a wayward game and poor distance control on his approach shots, fell by the wayside early, eventually shooting 76 and finishing tied for sixth with six others.

Mickelson, too, struggled. He shot 2-over-par 38 on his outward nine, with one birdie and three bogeys.

"I felt like I had hit a lot of good shots that led to bogeys," said Mickelson afterward. "When I made that putt on 10, that

Phil Mickelson watches as his tee shot on the par-5 15th hole rolls into the second cut on the left of the fairway.

gave me the momentum, if you will, to have a good back side."

The 12-foot par putt kept Mickelson in a tie at four-under-par with Bernhard Langer and only one stroke behind Els, who had posted an eagle, two birdies, and two bogeys for 34.

"It was a critical par," said the new Masters champion.

His brilliance took over from there, spinning off a series of deft shots that few have seen around these parts in a long time to the firm and fast greens.

Chris DiMarco pumps his fist in celebration after birdieing the second hole.

What They're Writing
(ROUND FOUR)

One of the most enthralling days in modern-day Masters history saw Phil Mickelson don his first Green Jacket, sinking a challenging 20-foot birdie putt on the last hole to edge out Ernie Els by a single stroke.

In the 67-year history of this tournament only three champions, Arnold Palmer, Sandy Lyle and Mark O'Meara, have clinched the title with a closing birdie, and Mickelson's 31 shots over the final nine holes—after almost losing touch with the leaders—will go down as one of the truly noteworthy comeback stories of Augusta National.

—*David Mackintosh,* Buenos Aires Herald

When the putt rolled in, and the gallery's impossible roar told his wife it was safe to open her eyes, Phil Mickelson jumped in the air like a child. He'd actually won the Masters, and done it the way a Masters should be won, with a 31 on the back nine and an 18-foot, tournament-winning putt.

Standing next to the 18th green, wearing a smile a dozen years in the making, Phil's father watched his son virtually dance to Butler Cabin to receive his Green Jacket.

Dad knew as well as anyone about the pain of being the best player to never win a major and the joy of shedding that burden forever.

—*Wright Thompson,* Kansas City Star

The newest Masters champion couldn't stop grinning. His wife couldn't stop crying.

"Is this real?" Amy Mickelson wondered.

It was easy to understand her confusion.

After 12 years of sticky failures and painful rationalizations, Phil Mickelson finally made his charge. Right up the back nine, where he lost the goat horns, the monkey and the shadow of a Tiger.

—*Dan Bickley,* Arizona Republic

Author Harry Gottlieb once claimed that "most golf pros would rather see a rattlesnake come up for a lesson than a southpaw." Such views require serious reappraisal, however, as Phil Mickelson threatens to maintain left-handed dominance of the Masters at Augusta National.

—*Dermot Gilleece,* Irish Independent

Korea's K. J. Choi tipped his hat to patrons after shooting a final round of 69 and finishing third.

A daring 8-iron to 12 feet on the 155-yard, par-3 12th hole began the string. Birdie.

"When I was on 12, just before I hit," said Mickelson, "I heard that Ernie had just made eagle. I heard the roar. I took a pretty aggressive line at that pin."

Because he's a left-hander, Mickelson knew that if he came out of the shot under pressure, it would likely drift left and away from a watery grave in Rae's Creek, the death knell of many a Masters contender

Shot of the Day

(ROUND FOUR)

Before the 2004 Masters, only three players had sunk a final birdie putt on the 72nd hole to win the Tournament. Arnold Palmer (1960), Sandy Lyle (1988), and Mark O'Meara (1998) were in rare company when Phil Mickelson joined them. Mickelson's winning birdie captured his first major. It came from 18 feet almost directly behind the hole, sliding down the slope, breaking right, and then turning imperceptibly back to the left before making a one-half turn around the lip and falling in. Mickelson watched his fellow competitor, Chris DiMarco, take the same line on a putt inches longer than his. DiMarco's putt broke away from the cup, but Mickelson's caught the corner of the hole and went in.

over time. The shot came off perfectly, drifting four yards left of the pin. Daring? Yes. Courageous? Certainly.

Els' 6-iron to 10 feet at No. 13 provided his second eagle of the day, pushing him three shots ahead of Mickelson before the birdie at No. 12.

A 7-iron from 195 yards on the par-5 13th hole allowed Mickelson to two-putt. Another birdie. Six under par. One behind Els.

A pitching wedge from 146 yards to

inches at the par-4 14th by Mickelson yielded another birdie.

Up ahead, Els birdied the par-5 15th. Advantage Els, by a stroke.

Mickelson counterpunched at the par-4 16th, using an 8-iron to 15 feet and dropping the putt. Tied.

When Els parred the final three holes, Mickelson's fate was squarely in his hands, and this time he grabbed the opportunity and didn't let go.

"You know I was trying to push," said Els

With a high, soft shot from the greenside bunker, Phil Mickelson got up-and-down for par on the fourth hole.

Ernie Els

(ROUND FOUR)

He didn't do what he set out to do.

Ernie Els did not win the 68th Masters Tournament.

Phil Mickelson did, birdieing the 72nd hole from 18 feet to win his first major.

Els, a 6-foot, 3-inch, 210-pound South African with an easygoing manner, watched another chance to win slip away.

Only this time it wasn't his fault.

He remembered the triple-bogey eight at the par-5 13th hole in the final round of 2002 that cost him a shot at the Masters title.

But this one hurt deeply, he said.

Els shot 67, establishing his best final-round Masters score. He shot 8-under-par 280, one stroke higher than in 2001, when he tied for sixth.

Yet this time Els' best wasn't good enough, and that nagged him.

He dearly wants a Masters title to add to his two U.S. Opens and one British Open. He wants it because he dearly loves the tradition of the Masters and its environment.

He wants it, too, because it would put him one step closer to a career Grand Slam, the act of winning all four majors. Els is missing the Masters and the PGA Championship.

To get so close the second week in April and to have it snatched away from you was painful, Els said.

That he had a three-shot lead midway through the second nine and still lost through no fault of his own didn't salve his wounds.

"You've done what you've done. I played as good as I could. What more can you do?" he said of the dramatic Mickelson finish, which included birdies on two of the last three holes.

"You know, it's disappointing. I've got to take stock after this. It's very tough for me to explain exactly what I feel right now."

Els' major disappointment came because of his Sunday shootout.

He made two eagles on par-5 holes and added three birdies and two bogeys, hardly the stuff one expects to add up to a second-place finish.

Golf is a cruel game, Els knows. But should it be this cruel?

"I gave it absolutely my best, especially today," he said. "But I'll get over this, no problem. I feel like I'll win a major this year. I would have loved to have won this one. I'm chasing that little Grand Slam a little bit in my career."

At 34 Els knows he's still in his prime, but winning Grand Slam events is never easy.

"I'll look myself in the mirror tonight and say, 'Well done,'" he said.

"I've had some good wins and I've had some tough losses and this is one of the tough losses."

Els acknowledged that Mickelson won the event with his brilliant play the final nine holes, when he shot 31. Fair enough, he said.

But it still hurt all the same.

South African Ernie Els wondered what was in store for him when the Masters ended.

PRIOR	HOLE	1	2	3	4	5	6	7
	PAR	4	5	4	3	4	3	4
6	DiMARCO	6	7	6	5	5	3	2
6	MICKELSON	6	7	6	6	5	4	4
4	CASEY	4	4	4	4	4	3	3
3	LANGER	4	5	5	4	4	4	3
3	ELS	3	4	3	3	2	2	3
3	CHOI	3	3	3	3	3	3	2
0	COUPLES	0	0	0	1	0	0	0
3	GARCIA	3	3	3	3	3	5	4
0	LOVE III	0	1	1	1	0	0	1
1	SINGH	1	0	0	1	1	1	1

LEADE

THRU 17

ELS	8
CHOI	6

A first-nine 39 Sunday took Chris DiMarco out of the title hunt, but he was able to finish tied for sixth.

of the pressure he applied to Mickelson on the second nine. "I was just trying to keep going."

Going wasn't Els' problem. Stopping Mickelson from going after his first major proved impossible.

"When I made that putt on 16, as I was walking up to the green, I really thought that it didn't seem overwhelming," said Mickelson. "I'll make this putt and I'll birdie one of the last two."

"He made birdie on 16," said Els of the 15-foot putt. "I heard that roar. And then obviously I could hear from the crowd's reaction, he hit it pretty close on 18 and then he made a great putt there."

Mickelson's game plan yielded a par at the 17th hole, leaving all the enormous Masters pressure squarely on his 6-foot-2, 190-pound frame.

Taking a 3-wood off the tee of the

Phil Mickelson stares at his tee shot at the par-3 fourth hole.

uphill, 465-yard, par-4 dogleg right hole, Mickelson found the left center of the fairway. His 8-iron above the pin left 18 feet between himself and immortality.

"Going into 18, with the pin being down left," said Mickelson, "I've seen a lot of guys birdie that last hole."

Maybe. But only three have done it to win the Masters—Arnold Palmer (1960), Sandy Lyle (1988), and Mark O'Meara (1998)—on the final putt.

Aided by a read of the putt from his fellow competitor Chris DiMarco, who was on the same line inches behind Mickelson's ball, one of the best putters on the PGA Tour set about cementing his long-awaited destiny.

"Because it was such a fast putt, I had a great look at his entire putt, every inch of the break," said Mickelson of DiMarco's putt.

"I gave it about six inches of break and it just hung on the edge."

As his putt crept agonizingly toward its target, Mickelson knew DiMarco's putt had broken left outside the hole and missed.

HOLE OF THE DAY
(ROUND FOUR)

HOLE NO. 14

Name: Chinese Fir

Par 4; 440 yards

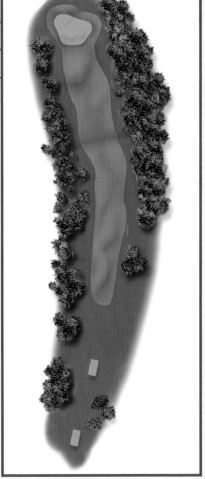

This hole didn't provide the ultimate drama that Phil Mickelson's winning putt at the 18th hole eventually would, but it provided the new champion with a key third birdie in a row. Mickelson, like five of the other 11 final-round leaders, birdied the hole. But he discussed the situation with his caddie, Jim MacKay, before settling the matter. They decided to hit a higher, fuller pitching wedge instead of a 9-iron, and it ended up within a foot of the hole location. The birdie pushed him to seven under par, proving that Mickelson's course management at a critical time was keenly accurate.

Did You Know?

Three holes-in-one—by Chris DiMarco, Padraig Harrington, and Kirk Triplett, the last two on No. 16 in the final round—set a record for the most aces in one Masters.

—

For the first time since the Masters Tournament began in 1934, the last six major championship winners have been first-timers. Masters champion Phil Mickelson joins Shaun Micheel (2003 PGA Championship), Ben Curtis (2003 British Open), Jim Furyk (2003 U.S. Open), Mike Weir (2003 Masters Tournament), and Rich Beem (2002 PGA Championship).

—

When amateur Casey Wittenberg of Memphis, Tennessee, finished in a four-way tie for 13th place at even-par 288, it marked the highest finish of a nonprofessional since Charles Coe finished T9 in 1962. Wittenberg recorded two eagles in his first Masters appearance.

—

Phil Mickelson's victory marked the first time that left-handed golfers have won the same major. Mike Weir won the Masters in 2003. Bob Charles is the only other left-hander to win a major championship, capturing the 1963 British Open.

—

The total number of 30 eagles for the 2004 Masters was the most since 32 in 1997. The 30 were also more than double the previous year's number, 13.

Chris DiMarco wasn't afraid to show his enthusiasm during the fourth round.

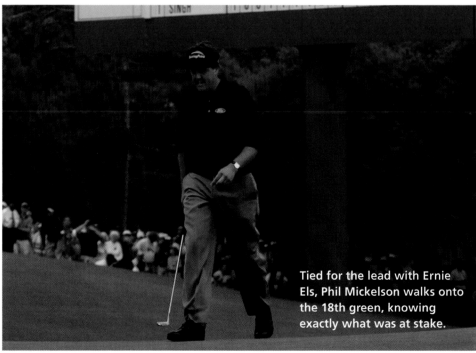

Tied for the lead with Ernie Els, Phil Mickelson walks onto the 18th green, knowing exactly what was at stake.

Mickelson's seemed headed for the same fate but it trickled right instead, curled halfway around the cup, and dropped in.

Fate? A higher being? Maybe, said Mickelson.

"I said earlier that my grandfather collects the flags of the tournaments that I win," he said. "And so I would save the flags. I'd write a little something on there and he would put them on his wall back home.

Before he died at 97 in January, Al Santos, Mickelson's grandfather, told the golfer he was tired of regular tournament flags. He wanted a major championship flag for his wall.

"I can't help but think that he may have had a little something to do with that [winning putt]," said the newest Masters champion.

With the victory, Mickelson has shown himself to be the best player in the game in 2004. He's won twice this year, none more important to him than the Masters.

"I have a memory or an experience that I'll remember for the rest of my life."

A few hours after his victory, when he was still having the traditional post-Masters dinner at the Club, thunder and rain fell loudly from the sky.

Some thought it might be Al Santos celebrating from the beyond.

After all, Grandpa now had that major championship flag, and Phil Mickelson had peace of mind.

Life couldn't be better. ∎

Allowing himself a broad smile despite the pressure, Phil Mickelson studies his birdie putt at No. 18.

Round Four LEADERS			1	2	3	4	5	6	7	8	9	Out	10	11	12	13	14	15	16	17	18	In	Rd4	Total
Pos.	Player	Par	4	5	4	3	4	3	4	5	4	36	4	4	3	5	4	5	3	4	4	36	72	
1	P. Mickelson	Score	4	4	5	3	5	4	4	5	4	38	4	4	2	4	3	5	2	4	3	31	69	279
		Status	−6	−7	−6	−6	−5	−4	−4	−4	−4		−4	−4	−5	−6	−7	−7	−8	−8	−9			
2	E. Els	Score	4	4	5	3	5	3	3	3	4	34	4	4	3	3	4	4	3	4	4	33	67	280
		Status	−3	−4	−3	−3	−2	−2	−3	−5	−5		−5	−5	−5	−7	−7	−8	−8	−8	−8			
3	K. J. Choi	Score	4	5	4	3	4	3	5	5	5	38	4	2	3	4	3	5	2	4	4	31	69	282
		Status	−3	−3	−3	−3	−3	−3	−2	−2	−1		−1	−3	−3	−4	−5	−5	−6	−6	−6			
T4	B. Langer	Score	3	4	4	4	4	3	5	4	4	35	4	4	3	5	3	7	2	5	4	37	72	285
		Status	−4	−5	−5	−4	−4	−4	−3	−4	−4		−4	−4	−4	−4	−5	−3	−4	−3	−3			
T4	S. Garcia	Score	4	5	4	3	4	5	3	4	3	35	4	4	2	4	5	3	2	3	4	31	66	285
		Status	+3	+3	+3	+3	+3	+5	+4	+3	+2		+2	+2	+1	E	+1	−1	−2	−3	−3			

Rounds	44
Below 70	8
Below par	18
Par	5
Over par	21
80+	0
Scoring average	72.546
Low score	66
Sergio Garcia	
High score	78
Tim Petrovic, Chris Riley	

Fourth-Round Stat
LEADERS

Driving distance
F. Couples, 320.0

Driving accuracy
C. Wittenberg, N. Price,
M. O'Meara, 12 of 14

Greens in regulation
S. Micheel, 14 of 18

Total putts
F. Jacobson, S. Cink,
J. Olazabal, 25

A wave of jubilation engulfs Phil Mickelson and patrons after his birdie putt fell into the cup.

Phil!

‖‖‖

When Phil Mickelson came to his 12th Masters Tournament, he was a confident, calculating golfer, a player who sensed this week would be different.

He came to his 12th Masters with a new sense of inner peace and bursting with confidence.

Phil Mickelson had already proven himself the best player in the first quarter of the PGA Tour season, with a win and seven top-10 finishes in eight events.

But the season's first major, at Augusta National Golf Club, was to be his litmus test. Mickelson, highly talented but known to have a gambler's philosophy in a game where patience, not recklessness, is a virtue, was a new, improved model.

Regardless of his inability to win one of the four Grand Slam events in his 12 years as a professional, the 33-year-old Californian knew his time would come. He had no doubt.

Maybe it was his record at the Masters.

He had finished third in each of the past three years prior to 2004 and rededicated himself to a strenuous off-season workout program and, coupled with hard work on his driving accuracy and short game, pushed himself into a Green Jacket.

"I had a different feeling playing this week," he said after his first major. "I just had a real belief that I was going to come through this week. I didn't want to get too excited because I had had that belief a number of times before and it never happened."

Even Mickelson's family noticed Phil's serene nature.

"I noticed that I was more relaxed," said Mickelson's father, Phil Sr. "I thought when he would hit the ball, it would be an odd thing if it wasn't right where he wanted it, on the fairway."

"There was a very different feeling in the air," said his sister, Tina, herself a teaching pro and television commentator. "All day we were telling each other, 'It's different this time; it's different today.' I know in hindsight it's easy to say this, but we knew he was going to win. There was no question about it."

Why now? Why at the Masters after all the years of near misses?

Perspective, perhaps.

Mickelson played poorly in 2003, failing to win for the first time since 1999. He was wayward with his driver and therefore

With a show of grand emotion, Phil Mickelson celebrates his first major title.

Phil Mickelson checks out the fit of his Green Jacket, a 43 long, as 2003 winner Mike Weir looks on.

sometimes wayward with his course management. One may have been the result of the other.

He worked with teacher Rick Smith to find more fairways, even at the risk of losing his prodigious distance. He worked on his short-game with Dave Pelz to hone his distance control on wedges.

He took a different look at his personal life after his wife, Amy, nearly died while giving birth to the couple's third child, Evan, in March 2003.

All those things changed Phil Mickelson and earned him the thing he wanted most: a major Tournament win at the Masters.

Statistically, his Masters performance was even better than the record he brought to the Tournament.

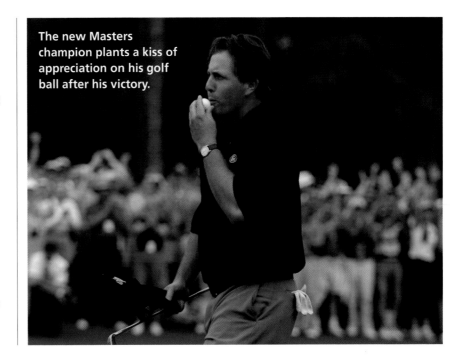

The new Masters champion plants a kiss of appreciation on his golf ball after his victory.

Chairman Hootie Johnson and Phil Mickelson both wore broad smiles at the presentation ceremony.

Mickelson hit 73.21 percent of his fairways at Augusta National Golf Club, up nearly 10 percent from his 2004 PGA Tour figures and drastically up from his 49 percent rate in 2003. He hit 53 of 72 greens in regulation for a 73.61 percentage, the best of anyone in the field, nearly 10 percent better than in his 2003 season.

All that allowed Mickelson to avoid the bane of Masters pretenders—the big number. His only double bogey came on the par-3 16th hole in the first round. He played the last 36 holes six under par, with only three bogeys.

Masterful? You bet.

Is Mickelson a different person than a year ago?

"I'm certainly happier," he said.

A Masters victory will do that. ▮

Low amateur Casey Wittenberg shared his thoughts with Masters officials and patrons at the presentation ceremony.

Chairman Hootie Johnson presents 2004 champion Phil Mickelson with a sterling replica of the Masters Trophy.

Results & Statistics

—— ||| ——

Player	Position	Scores	Total	Money
Phil Mickelson	1	72 69 69 69	279	$1,170,000
Low Professional: Gold Medal				
Sterling Silver Replica Masters Trophy				
Ernie Els (South Africa)	2	70 72 71 67	280	$702,000
Runner-up: Silver Medal				
Sterling Silver Salver				
Pair of Crystal Goblets, Eagle, Round 4, Hole 8				
Pair of Crystal Goblets, Eagle, Round 4, Hole 13				
K. J. Choi (Korea)	3	71 70 72 69	282	$442,000
Pair of Crystal Goblets, Eagle, Round 4, Hole 11				
Sergio Garcia (Spain)	T4	72 72 75 66	285	$286,000
Crystal Vase, Day's Low Score (66), Round 4				
Pair of Crystal Goblets, Eagle, Round 1, Hole 15				
Pair of Crystal Goblets, Eagle, Round 4, Hole 15				
Bernhard Langer (Germany)	T4	71 73 69 72	285	$286,000
Pair of Crystal Goblets, Eagle, Round 3, Hole 15				
Paul Casey (England)	T6	75 69 68 74	286	$189,893
Fred Couples	T6	73 69 74 70	286	$189,893
Chris DiMarco	T6	69 73 68 76	286	$189,893
Crystal Bowl, Hole-in-One, Round 1, Hole 6				
Davis Love III	T6	75 67 74 70	286	$189,893
Crystal Vase, Day's Low Score (67), Round 2				
Pair of Crystal Goblets, Eagle, Round 2, Hole 15				
Nick Price (Zimbabwe)	T6	72 73 71 70	286	$189,893
Vijay Singh (Fiji)	T6	75 73 69 69	286	$189,893
Pair of Crystal Goblets, Eagle, Round 3, Hole 2				
Kirk Triplett	T6	71 74 69 72	286	$189,893
Crystal Bowl, Hole-in-One, Round 4, Hole 16				
Retief Goosen (South Africa)	T13	75 73 70 70	288	$125,667
Pair of Crystal Goblets, Eagle, Round 4, Hole 2				
Padraig Harrington (Ireland)	T13	74 74 68 72	288	$125,667
Crystal Bowl, Hole-in-One, Round 4, Hole 16				
Charles Howell III	T13	71 71 76 70	288	$125,667

Player	Position	Scores	Total	Money
Casey Wittenberg	T13	76 72 71 69	288	Amateur
Low Amateur: Sterling Silver Cup				
Pair of Crystal Goblets, Eagle, Round 3, Hole 10				
Pair of Crystal Goblets, Eagle, Round 4, Hole 15				
Stewart Cink	T17	74 73 69 73	289	$97,500
Steve Flesch	T17	76 67 77 69	289	$97,500
Crystal Vase, Day's Low Score (67), Round 2				
Pair of Crystal Goblets, Eagle, Round 2, Hole 15				
Jay Haas	T17	69 75 72 73	289	$97,500
Fredrik Jacobson (Sweden)	T17	74 74 67 74	289	$97,500
Crystal Vase, Day's Low Score (67), Round 3				
Stephen Leaney (Australia)	T17	76 71 73 69	289	$97,500
Pair of Crystal Goblets, Eagle, Round 2, Hole 8				
Pair of Crystal Goblets, Eagle, Round 4, Hole 13				
Stuart Appleby (Australia)	T22	73 74 73 70	290	$70,200
Pair of Crystal Goblets, Eagle, Round 3, Hole 15				
Pair of Crystal Goblets, Eagle, Round 4, Hole 2				
Shaun Micheel	T22	72 76 72 70	290	$70,200
Pair of Crystal Goblets, Eagle, Round 4, Hole 2				
Justin Rose (England)	T22	67 71 81 71	290	$70,200
Crystal Vase, Day's Low Score (67), Round 1				
Pair of Crystal Goblets, Eagle, Round 4, Hole 8				
Tiger Woods	T22	75 69 75 71	290	$70,200
Alexander Cejka (Germany)	26	70 70 78 73	291	$57,200
Pair of Crystal Goblets, Eagle, Round 1, Hole 13				
Mark O'Meara	T27	73 70 75 74	292	$51,025
Pair of Crystal Goblets, Eagle, Round 2, Hole 15				
Bob Tway	T27	75 71 74 72	292	$51,025
Scott Verplank	29	74 71 76 72	293	$48,100
José Maria Olazabal (Spain)	30	71 69 79 75	294	$46,150
Pair of Crystal Goblets, Eagle, Round 2, Hole 13				
Bob Estes	T31	76 72 73 74	295	$41,275

Phil Mickelson has his Green Jacket adjusted by 2003 champion Mike Weir following the presentation ceremony.

Player	Position	Scores	Total	Money
Brad Faxon	T31	72 76 76 71	295	$41,275
Pair of Crystal Goblets, Eagle, Round 3, Hole 15				
Jerry Kelly	T31	74 72 73 76	295	$41,275
Ian Poulter (England)	T31	75 73 74 73	295	$41,275
Justin Leonard	T35	76 72 72 76	296	$35,913
Phillip Price (Wales)	T35	71 76 73 76	296	$35,913
Paul Lawrie (Scotland)	T37	77 70 73 77	297	$32,663
Sandy Lyle (Scotland)	T37	72 74 75 76	297	$32,663
Eduardo Romero (Argentina)	39	74 73 74 77	298	$30,550
Todd Hamilton	40	77 71 76 75	299	$29,250
Pair of Crystal Goblets, Eagle, Round 2, Hole 13				
Tim Petrovic	T41	72 75 75 78	300	$27,950
Brandt Snedeker	T41	73 75 75 77	300	Amateur
Low Amateur Runner-up: Silver Medal				
Jeff Sluman	43	73 70 82 77	302	$26,650
Chris Riley	44	70 78 78 78	304	$25,350
Robert Allenby (Australia)	–	73 76 – –	149	$5,000
Michael Campbell (New Zealand)	–	76 73 – –	149	$5,000
Darren Clarke (N. Ireland)	–	70 79 – –	149	$5,000
Ben Crenshaw	–	74 75 – –	149	$5,000
John Daly	–	78 71 – –	149	$5,000
Raymond Floyd	–	73 76 – –	149	$5,000
J. L. Lewis	–	77 72 – –	149	$5,000
Pair of Crystal Goblets, Eagle, Round 2, Hole 2				
Peter Lonard (Australia)	–	74 75 – –	149	$5,000
Craig Perks (New Zealand)	–	76 73 – –	149	$5,000
John Rollins	–	74 75 – –	149	$5,000
Craig Stadler	–	74 75 – –	149	$5,000
Mike Weir (Canada)	–	79 70 – –	149	$5,000
Lian-Wei Zhang (China)	–	77 72 – –	149	$5,000
Pair of Crystal Goblets, Eagle, Round 2, Hole 13				
Briny Baird	–	77 73 – –	150	$5,000
Rich Beem	–	77 73 – –	150	$5,000
Ben Curtis	–	73 77 – –	150	$5,000
Pair of Crystal Goblets, Eagle, Round 1, Hole 7				
Fred Funk	–	80 70 – –	150	$5,000

Player	Position	Scores	Total	Money
Jeff Maggert	–	78 72 – –	150	$5,000
Larry Mize	–	76 74 – –	150	$5,000
Jack Nicklaus	–	75 75 – –	150	$5,000
Craig Parry (Australia)	–	74 76 – –	150	$5,000
Nathan Smith	–	78 72 – –	150	Amateur
Angel Cabrera (Argentina)	–	74 77 – –	151	$5,000
Nick Faldo (England)	–	76 75 – –	151	$5,000
Jonathan Kaye	–	79 72 – –	151	$5,000
Len Mattiace	–	76 75 – –	151	$5,000
Rocco Mediate	–	75 76 – –	151	$5,000
Colin Montgomerie (Scotland)	–	71 80 – –	151	$5,000
David Toms	–	78 73 – –	151	$5,000
Ian Woosnam (Wales)	–	76 75 – –	151	$5,000
Nick Flanagan (Australia)	–	78 74 – –	152	Amateur
Toshi Izawa (Japan)	–	76 76 – –	152	$5,000
Kenny Perry	–	74 78 – –	152	$5,000
Tom Watson	–	76 76 – –	152	$5,000
Pair of Crystal Goblets, Eagle, Round 2, Hole 13				
Jonathan Byrd	–	79 74 – –	153	$5,000
Chad Campbell	–	76 77 – –	153	$5,000
Trevor Immelman (South Africa)	–	77 76 – –	153	$5,000
Shigeki Maruyama (Japan)	–	82 71 – –	153	$5,000
Adam Scott (Australia)	–	80 73 – –	153	$5,000
Gary Wolstenholme (England)	–	77 76 – –	153	Amateur
Tim Clark (South Africa)	–	73 81 – –	154	$5,000
Tim Herron	–	80 74 – –	154	$5,000
Brian Davis (England)	–	82 73 – –	155	$5,000
Thomas Bjorn (Denmark)	–	80 77 – –	157	$5,000
Fuzzy Zoeller	–	79 81 – –	160	$5,000
Gary Player (South Africa)	–	82 80 – –	162	$5,000
Charles Coody	–	88 79 – –	167	$5,000
Arnold Palmer	–	84 84 – –	168	$5,000
Tommy Aaron	–	87 83 – –	170	$5,000

			TOTAL	$6,286,050

Final
SCORING

Rounds	274
Below 70	27
Below par	67
Par	27
Over par	180
80+	18
Scoring average	73.974
Low score	Sergio Garcia, Round 4, 66
High score	Charles Coody, Round 1, 88

Final Stat
LEADERS

Driving distance
F. Couples, 301.13 yards

Driving accuracy
J. Kelly, 47 of 56

Greens in regulation
P. Mickelson, 53 of 72

Total putts
S. Appleby, J. Olazabal, 109

Keeping patrons up to date on the Tournament's progress is a continual job at the main scoreboard.

FINAL COURSE STATISTICS

Hole	Yards	Par	Average	Rank*	Eagles	Birdies	Pars	Bogeys	Double Bogeys	Others
1	435	4	4.354	1	0	13	165	85	8	3
2	575	5	4.774	18	5	81	162	24	1	1
3	350	4	4.029	14	0	39	192	39	4	0
4	205	3	3.245	5	0	13	188	67	5	1
5	455	4	4.277	4	0	20	167	79	7	1
6	180	3	3.175	10	1	24	186	52	11	0
7	410	4	4.088	12	1	44	160	68	1	0
8	570	5	4.832	15	3	72	172	22	5	0
9	460	4	4.124	11	0	35	180	51	6	2
Out	3640	36	36.898		10	341	1572	487	48	8
10	495	4	4.186	8	1	21	188	55	8	1
11	490	4	4.292	3	1	19	165	78	10	1
12	155	3	3.186	9	0	42	168	41	19	4
13	510	5	4.825	16	7	89	135	31	12	0
14	440	4	4.226	6	0	27	169	67	11	0
15	500	5	4.785	17	9	90	137	30	6	2
16	170	3	3.036	13	2	47	169	51	5	0
17	425	4	4.193	7	0	26	182	55	9	2
18	465	4	4.347	2	0	20	156	84	11	3
In	3650	36	37.076		20	381	1469	492	91	13
Total	7290	72	73.974		30	722	3041	979	139	21

*Holes ranked from 1 (most difficult) to 18 (least difficult).

All-Time Scoring Records

Low First Nine
30, Johnny Miller, third round, 1975
30, Greg Norman, fourth round, 1988
30, K. J. Choi, second round, 2004

Low Second Nine
29, Mark Calcavecchia, fourth round, 1992
29, David Toms, fourth round, 1998

Low 18
63 (33–30), Nick Price, third round, 1986
63 (33–30), Greg Norman, first round, 1996

Low First Round
63 (33–30), Greg Norman, 1996

Low Second Round
64 (31–33), Miller Barber, 1979
64 (33–31), Jay Haas, 1995

Low Third Round
63 (33–30), Nick Price, 1986

Low Fourth Round
64 (34–30), Maurice Bembridge, 1974
64 (32–32), Hale Irwin, 1975
64 (34–30), Gary Player, 1978
64 (30–34), Greg Norman, 1988
64 (35–29), David Toms, 1998

Low First 36 Holes
131 (65–66), Raymond Floyd, 1976

Low Middle 36 Holes
131 (66–65), Tiger Woods, 1997

Low Last 36 Holes
131 (65–66), Johnny Miller, 1975

Low First 54 Holes
201 (65–66–70), Raymond Floyd, 1976
201 (70–66–65), Tiger Woods, 1997

Low Last 54 Holes
200 (66–65–69), Tiger Woods, 1997

Low 72 Holes
270 (70–66–65–69), Tiger Woods, 1997

Highest Winning Score
289, Sam Snead, 1954
289, Jack Burke, 1956

Low 18-Hole Score by a First-Year Player
64 (32–32), Lloyd Mangrum, first round, 1940
64 (31–33), Mike Donald, first round, 1990
64 (35–29), David Toms, fourth round, 1998

Low 72 Holes by a First-Year Player
278 (71–66–74–67), Toshi Izawa, 2001

Low 18 by an Amateur
66 (32–34), Ken Venturi, first round, 1956

Low 72 Holes by an Amateur
281 (72–71–69–69), Charles R. Coe, 1961

SCORING SUMMARY

	Below 70	Under Par	Par	Over Par	80 & Over	Course Average	Round Leader	Low Round	Phil Mickelson
Round 1	3	14	7	72	10	75.173	Justin Rose (67)	Justin Rose (67)	T15
Round 2	7	22	11	60	6	73.784	Justin Rose (138)	Davis Love (67) Steve Flesch (67)	T4
Round 3	9	13	4	27	2	73.272	Chris DiMarco (210) Phil Mickelson (210)	Fredrick Jacobson (67)	T1
Round 4	8	18	15	21	0	72.546	Phil Mickelson (279)	Sergio Garcia (66)	1
All Rounds	27	67	27	180	18	73.974			

Past Champions

'04	Phil Mickelson	279	'68	Bob Goalby	277
'03	Mike Weir	281	'67	Gay Brewer	280
'02	Tiger Woods	276	'66	Jack Nicklaus	288
'01	Tiger Woods	272	'65	Jack Nicklaus	271
'00	Vijay Singh	278	'64	Arnold Palmer	276
'99	José Maria Olazabal	280	'63	Jack Nicklaus	286
'98	Mark O'Meara	279	'62	Arnold Palmer	280
'97	Tiger Woods	270	'61	Gary Player	280
'96	Nick Faldo	276	'60	Arnold Palmer	282
'95	Ben Crenshaw	274	'59	Art Wall	284
'94	José Maria Olazabal	279	'58	Arnold Palmer	284
'93	Bernhard Langer	277	'57	Doug Ford	283
'92	Fred Couples	275	'56	Jack Burke	289
'91	Ian Woosnam	277	'55	Cary Middlecoff	279
'90	Nick Faldo	278	'54	Sam Snead	289
'89	Nick Faldo	283	'53	Ben Hogan	274
'88	Sandy Lyle	281	'52	Sam Snead	286
'87	Larry Mize	285	'51	Ben Hogan	280
'86	Jack Nicklaus	279	'50	Jimmy Demaret	283
'85	Bernhard Langer	282	'49	Sam Snead	282
'84	Ben Crenshaw	277	'48	Claude Harmon	279
'83	Seve Ballesteros	280	'47	Jimmy Demaret	281
'82	Craig Stadler	284	'46	Herman Keiser	282
'81	Tom Watson	280	'45	No tournament, WWII	
'80	Seve Ballesteros	275	'44	No tournament, WWII	
'79	Fuzzy Zoeller	280	'43	No tournament, WWII	
'78	Gary Player	277	'42	Byron Nelson	280
'77	Tom Watson	276	'41	Craig Wood	280
'76	Raymond Floyd	271	'40	Jimmy Demaret	280
'75	Jack Nicklaus	276	'39	Ralph Guldahl	279
'74	Gary Player	278	'38	Henry Picard	285
'73	Tommy Aaron	283	'37	Byron Nelson	283
'72	Jack Nicklaus	286	'36	Horton Smith	285
'71	Charles Coody	279	'35	Gene Sarazen	282
'70	Billy Casper	279	'34	Horton Smith	284
'69	George Archer	281			

Phil Mickelson at the Masters

Year	Position	Rounds	Total	Money
1991	T46	69 73 74 74	290	Amateur
1993	T34	72 71 75 73	291	$8,975
1995	T7	66 71 70 73	280	$70,950
1996	3	65 73 72 72	282	$170,000
1997	MC	76 74	150	$5,000
1998	T12	74 69 69 74	286	$64,800
1999	T6	74 69 71 71	285	$125,200
2000	T7	71 68 76 71	286	$143,367
2001	3	67 69 69 70	275	$380,800
2002	3	69 72 68 71	280	$380,800
2003	3	73 70 72 68	283	$408,000
2004	1	72 69 69 69	279	$1,170,000

Masters Club Dinner

— III —

Front Row (left to right): Jack Burke, Arnold Palmer, Byron Nelson, Mike Weir, Chairman Hootie Johnson, Doug Ford. *Second Row:* Craig Stadler, Tiger Woods, Fred Couples, Bernhard Langer, Bob Goalby, Jack Nicklaus, Gay Brewer, Billy Casper, Raymond Floyd, Nick Faldo. *Third Row:* Vijay Singh, George Archer, Ben Crenshaw, Tom Watson, José Maria Olazabal, Sandy Lyle, Larry Mize, Mark O'Meara, Gary Player, Ian Woosnam, Fuzzy Zoeller, Charles Coody.

Amateur Dinner

Left to right: Casey Wittenberg, Brandt Snedeker, Chairman Hootie Johnson, Gary Wolstenholme, Nathan Smith, Nick Flanagan.

Committee Chairmen

Front Row (left to right): George R. Wislar, John H. Dobbs, Eugene M. Howerdd Jr., Edwin L. Douglass Jr., Phil S. Harison, Chairman Hootie Johnson, Joe T. Ford, James E. Johnson Jr., Charles H. Morris, J. Haley Roberts Jr. *Back Row:* William P. Payne, Ogden M. Phipps, W. Lipscomb Davis Jr., Leroy H. Simkins Jr., William T. Gary III, Will F. Nicholson Jr., Dr. H. Ray Finney, John W. Harris, H. Lawrence Parker, John L. Murray Jr., Frank Troutman Jr.

Rules Committee

Front Row (left to right): Emily Crisp, Irving Fish, Jeremy N. Caplan, Peter Dawson, Mary Bea Porter-King, Gordon B. B. Jeffrey, Fred S. Ridley, Will F. Nicholson Jr., HRH The Duke of York KCVO ADC, Eugene M. Howerdd Jr., Thomas J. Meeks, John D. Reynolds III. *Second Row:* Bruce C. Richards, Craig Ammerman, Andrew Langford-Jones, David J. Harrison, Andy Yamanaka, Theo Manyama, Mike Shea, Loren Singletary, James E. Reinhart, Stephen Ross, Bruce Sudderth, Paul D. Caruso Jr., Jack Connelly, Sir Michael Bonallack, Roger Warren. *Third Row:* David Pepper, Robert H. Chapman III, David B. Fay, Ed Hoard, James B. Hyler Jr., Michael B. Brown, Fredric C. Nelson, David E. Rickman, Stephen Cox, Sue Ewart, Harry W. Easterly Jr., C. Jay Rains, M. G. Orender, Don Essig III, Mark Wilson, Jesse Barge, Dow Finsterwald, Charles Lanzetta. *Fourth Row:* James J. A. Halliday, James T. Bunch, Lew Blakey, David Price, Thomas O'Toole Jr., Miguel Vidaor, F. Morgan Taylor Jr., Benjamin F. Nelson, H. Colin Maclaine, James F. Vernon, Brian Whitcomb, John Paramor, Andy McFee, John Brendle, Joe E. Black, Jamie Conkling, Mark Russell, Gene Smith.

Golf Writers Association of America

Front Row (left to right): Carlos Monarrez, Tod Leonard, Jack Berry, Don Thompson, George Willis, Lew Hege, David Mackintosh, Richard Mudry, Tom Auclair, Reiko Takekawa, Sadao Iwata, Kaye Kessler, Gary Van Sickle, George Sweda, Vartan Kupelian, Joe Gordon, Marino Parascenzo, Melanie Hauser. *Second Row:* Peter Kerasotis, Joel Walker, James Achenbach, Bud Thompson, Chuck Harty, Brian Murphy, Ed Sherman, Bill Fields, Mark Herrmann, Reid Spencer, Neil Geoghegan, Greg Johnson, George Kimball, Sal Johnson. *Third Row:* Tommy Snell, Nura Pastor, David Califa, John Steinbreder, Scott Macpherson, Steve Hershey, Len Shapiro, Byron Huff, Ryan Herrington, Hank Gola, Mike Kern, Joe Juliano, Mike Dudurich, Gerry Dulac, Dave Hackenberg. *Fourth Row:* Furman Bisher, Jim McCabe, Doug Ferguson, Mike Buteau, John Davis, Dave Perkins, Larry Dorman, Jaime Diaz, Dave Shedloski, Ken Bowden, Adam Schupak, Roger Graves, Tom Mackin, Tom Kensler. *Fifth Row:* Nick Seitz, Art Spander, Dove Jones, Glenn Sheeley, Craig Dolch, Jeff Shain, Steve Campbell, Joe Logan, Helen Ross, Joe Tomlinson, Gordon Wells, Jack Bacot, Alan Blondin, Bruce Berlet. *Sixth Row:* Michael Vegis, Ann Liguori, Mick Elliott, Dana von Louda, Steve Elling, Clifton Brown, Robert Hartman, John Boyette, Chuck Cavalaris, Jeff Waters, Ken Carpenter, Carol Hall, Joe Hall, Pete Georgiady, Dick Donovan, Larry Durland, Dave Pelz, Bruce Vittner, Todd Vasey, Eddie Pelz.